A REPUBLIC OF EQUALS

A
Republic
of
Equals

★ ★ ★ ★ ★

BY
LESLIE W. DUNBAR

Ann Arbor

The University of Michigan Press

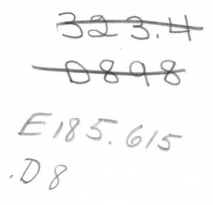

To My Wife

Preface

This is not a book about civil rights, about the Negro revolt, or about the South. I have tried, rather, to estimate what they have meant, in their combined impact, to this country and to some of its political ideas and institutions. This has been one of the truly profound and nation-shaking chapters of our history. To do well what I have attempted here would require both much more space and a longer time perspective than I have used. So this is at most and at best a sketch of probabilities.

The book proceeds, as any such book would need to do, on several levels of interpretation and inquiry. All of these are, however, subordinate to one connecting theme which is that the civil-rights movement and the reforms coming from it are the culmination of a liberal era which began with the great Depression. Civil rights was the final item implied on the agenda of modern liberalism. With the significant attainment of constitutional rights, the old liberal program is closed and liberals now have responsibilities of rule (and must, therefore, in considerable measure concede their ancient function of social criticism to others).

But the Negro revolt not only fulfills an era. It has introduced another. Integration is a greater thing than civil rights. Will the liberals who now rule this country have the resources of energy and mind to meet its requirements? Can they take the giant step President Johnson proposed in June 1965 at Howard University, when he said that the liberal goal of equal opportunity is not enough and that we must achieve equal results?

The lesser themes in the book start with the South and its key importance within the republic's constitutional order. Since the plane of discourse is throughout political, this leads to discussions of the resiliency and future worth of federalism. Questions as basic as these must be faced in the wake of a movement that forces on the American people, as nothing else in our history so urgently has done, a painful yet wonderful revaluation of its society and its premises. The final gift of the Negro revolt may be that it will bring the nation to the maturity of self-examination and self-discovery.

The five essays of this book were originally so many lectures, given as the William W. Cook Lectures on American Institutions at The University of Michigan, October 19–November 2, 1965. For the many kindnesses of the University, the Cook Committee, and the University of Michigan Press I am genuinely appreciative. Several friends, each deeply engaged in the civil-rights movement, have read and criticized the manuscript. They have helped me greatly to tighten its arguments, though disagreeing sharply with some of them.

Finally, whatever general strengths the book may have are attributable to the opportunity I was given from 1959–65 to work with the Southern Regional Council. No man could have had richer associations during those years. I can only hope that these good friends—Negro and white Southerners—will find the book somewhat worthy of the instruction they gave me.

LESLIE W. DUNBAR

Pelham, New York

Contents

I

★ ★ ★ ★ ★

The Republic Accepts Its Constitution

On February 1, 1956, the General Assembly of Virginia adopted a resolution interposing its authority against the school desegregation decision of the Supreme Court of the United States. The resolution announced "that until the question here asserted by the State of Virginia be settled by clear Constitutional amendment, we pledge our firm intention to take all appropriate measures honorably, legally, and constitutionally available to us, to resist this illegal encroachment upon our sovereign powers."

The next day, the Legislature of Alabama declared that "the decisions and order of the Supreme Court of the United States relating to separation of races in the public schools are, as a matter of fact, null, void, and of no effect; and the Legislature of Alabama declares to all men, as a matter of right, this State is not bound to abide thereby." Resolutions similar to these two were at later dates adopted in all southern states except Tennessee and Texas.

On March 12, 1956, nineteen senators from the Southern states—all except Senator Lyndon B. Johnson of Texas and Senators Kefauver and Gore of Tennessee—joined with eighty-two Southern representatives in introducing a Declaration of Constitutional Principles, popularly known as the "Southern Manifesto." They held that "this unwarranted exercise of power by the Court, contrary to the Constitution, is creating chaos and confusion in the states principally affected," and proceeded to "commend the motives of those states which have declared the intention to resist forced integration by any lawful means."

The years following have been for the federal system of the United States a time of unique and strenuous trial; for the American people they have been a long enduring upheaval. The end of it all is not yet in sight, though the character of the trial has changed, from a contest regarding the distribution of powers within the federal system to the question of how well the federal structure and how well the people can cope with the problems that all along underlay that contest.

These have been years of test and of revelation. It is possible that no men like those who bombed the Birmingham church on a spring Sunday morning in 1963, or who burned and frenziedly looted throughout a Los Angeles weekend in 1965, ever before appeared in this nation in quite the same character, or will ever again. In their time they were here, however, and they and their time were the yield of all our history. Good has not the same inevitability as evil, but in these same years and from this same history came people who brought new richness, new stamina to the national character, and showed courage in a different and more humane aspect than we had known it before. These have been years of learning about ourselves, and of what we are capable.

We Americans have, of course, always been curious about ourselves. Not until recently, though, has curiosity trespassed old ground rules that protected us from basically disturbing findings. From time to time aberrant ancestors had questioned the integrity of the American experience, but neither they nor more heavy-handed detractors from abroad were able to spoil the nation's profound certainty of its moral soundness and political and economic superiority; foreign critics, in fact, had an accepted role in American life—a class of entertainers whom we paid and by and large enjoyed.

All has changed. Domestic critics are now legion, and their output is the stuff on which book clubs prosper. Foreign critics still entertain, though they become less easy to enjoy as their numbers multiply, their art erodes, and their wares descend from literature to anthropology. These inflictions on our self-assurance and self-satisfaction are light, however, compared with the information stored up each day in our consciousness that we are crazily involved in affairs all over the world and that despite or because of our stupendous power we are widely disliked and often ferociously hated.

Yet we owe even more to Negro Americans than to forces abroad for our unfolding self-discovery, for the Negro revolt led American democracy into a room of mirrors, and what we saw was everywhere soiled and here and there so decayed as to be vile. We saw ourselves. Vividly if not always clearly we saw unwanted scenes of national life and the lacerated purposes of our individual existences.

The self-examination in which we are now engaged, brought on by our worldwide exposure as well as the Negro revolt, may be one of the truly necessary frontiers that Americans pass through and occupy and make a home in. We are, perhaps, a new genus of Americans—the very first to be cut off from the national legacy of self-satisfaction.

The civil-rights movement, at its beginning, did not promise to contribute to such an end. Nor did it then seem to embody great challenges to the governmental order. It began with issues so simple that we thought a court decree or an executive order could adequately solve them. We have come to see that the very nature of our constitution is the true issue. This is so if we think of the constitution as that set of legal norms which is this country's highest enforceable statute. But it is so in even greater measure if we think of the constitution in the older significance of the word.

A constitution, Aristotle taught, is the organization and distribution of authority within a society in order to accord with and express "the way of life of a citizen-body." Legal norms are merely its attributes. In this Aristotelian sense, we might say that the real American constitution is the manner in which the respective interests of businesses, labor, agriculture, and the professions are distributed and articulated. But, also, because this is America with its peculiar history, the constitution has valued not only these interests but also those of the white race and those of something called "the South."

This actual constitution has been inherently unstable, for by making the white race privileged it introduced gradation of citizenship, and Aristotle long ago had observed that that was a fatal flaw in any constitution.[1] If we were capable of the dispassionate honesty of an Aristotle or a Machiavelli, we might observe that our policies toward the American Indians, whose life today is perhaps even more miserable than that of Negro Americans, were practical. They have prevented the Indians from becoming as yet a cause of constitutional instability; we exterminated hordes of them, we forced the remnants to live together in isolated places, and we did not depend on them economically. We not only rendered them weak, but we denied them all but the tiniest shreds of an opportunity to become strong.

Our ancestors' policy toward Negroes was almost the reverse. They did not practice mass killings, they mingled Negroes among whites, and they made economic use of Negroes. When they did this, they built within our constitution an imbalance that had to be, in time, rectified.

This imbalance was made more ponderous by the irrational acceptance, after about 1825, of the entity called "the South" as one of the interests which had privileges which the constitution must recognize and

[1]For this and the preceding reference to Aristotle, citations are to *Politics*, 1295a, 1281b.

support. The veto power of "the South" has been as real a part of our constitution as any other element in it.

Our constitution is being reshaped. At the least, certain of the legal norms have been bent or been replaced by others, and more of this will likely occur. The veto power of "the South" is finally being erased, and if the nation had no reason other than this to be grateful to the Negro movement its debt would still be huge. At the optimum, the reshaping may invalidate the old rule and privilege of color. At the worst, we may exchange the veto power of "the South" in our constitution for the veto power of Negroes.

The Negro movement is invested, therefore, not only with concern for Negroes, but with concern for the constitution, both the legal and the real. None has perhaps envisioned this more clearly than two groups near the opposite ends of the spectrum of controversy. The young radicals of the civil-rights movement have, with keener realism than their elders, known that integration is an impossibility without decisive and large alterations in the social system. And Southern segregationists have not generally been sick minds, as one so often hears them described, but realists, because they have known with the same clarity as the young radicals that a way of life is at stake.

For Americans of a generation or even a decade ago to think clearly about the Negro problem was quite impossible. I cannot recall a single commentator, no matter how gifted, who had the understanding which we have today. This is not due to our intellectual merits, but to the fact that the Negro revolt has bridged over a mass of mental sets which we could not penetrate by thought.

When we tried to think through it, we were held in a swamp formed by the seepage from our own minds and culture. For some few like Faulkner, the swamp was a still and quiet place of meditation, as good a place as any and better than most for searching out the strengths of mankind. For most of us it was a mire to be avoided, with some pain of conscience but with greater relief. The swamp was made up of all those catechetical responses we had so often uttered and so little understood about federalism and state rights and local self-government; of judicial precedents like the *Civil Rights Cases* and *Plessy* v. *Ferguson* and *Grovey* v. *Townsend,* where just thirty years ago the Supreme Court of the United States upheld the white primary; of moral shorthand like "you can't legislate morals" and "we must change hearts and minds" and "extremists on both sides"; of glib assumption that politics is the art of the possible and no effort is worthwhile because, against the power of the South, none can succeed. The bog was knotted with Biblical texts and an evangelical religion; with the example of the churches and the nonconcern of their preachers and bishops; with the imperturbability of their congregations. It was deepened by what we thought or believed we thought about property rights; about craft unionism; about the need, if we were Jewish or Catholic or labor unionist, to advance ourselves and be careful of giving offense. The swamp was darkened by mists of lingering social Darwinism; by the gospel of the white man's burden; by the testimony of anthropologists that black men were inferior; by our own suspicion that this was so, because, unless we lived in the South, the only ones we were likely to see were the dancing, killing African savages the movies liked to present or Stepinfetchit types that both the movies and the street called forth: all others were invisible men; and, if we lived in the South, all the Negroes we saw acted as if they thought themselves inferior and the ones who wouldn't act that obscene way stayed removed from white people. The currents in the swamp ran slowly, with little or no force, because there were so relatively few Negroes anywhere except in the South, where they didn't count, and in legendary, mysterious places like Harlem. And all around were pockets of intellectual quicksand: the sentimentalizing of the South by the rest of the nation, secret admiration vying with habitual public disapproval; deviously intricate patterns of ingrained, unthought behavior; and, though chiefly in the southern end of the swamp, many genuine and soul-troubling and affectionate and even loving attachments of individual Negroes and whites, balanced by a Negro-hating meanness that was, and is, more ethically appalling than the frequent lynchings.

The nation could hardly think and could not act. Then the Negro movement cut through the swamp and ended the nation's paralysis. White America may now flagellate itself with feelings of guilt and Negro America may accuse, and possibly some net gain in morality will come from this, though that is far from certain. The concept of collective guilt is an effusion of neurotically escapist minds. The day of reform had had to wait on leadership strong and secure enough to sweep away the debris of 350 years of history. That leadership came from the only persons who could provide it, from the only Americans not mired in the swamp, from Negro Americans themselves.

When the nation was confronted by the so-called "Negro revolt," when the nation finally in 1960 began to turn and face it, it confronted a lot else besides. Given the fact that we are a nation slow to learn, we learned fairly quickly what the Southern segregationists had known all along. We learned that civil rights for Negroes would change our way of life *unless* we could make accommodations in the social system with enough skill and of enough size so as both to preserve our institutions and the essential spirit of our culture and to satisfy the just demands of all citizens.

We had done this before. Edward S. Corwin, in one of his best-known books, *Constitutional Revolution Ltd.*, wrote an apt description of what the New Deal achieved by way of both preservation and innovation. In a letter to me in 1956, Dr. Corwin remarked, with characteristic emphasis, on the stupidity of the South, particularly Virginia, and then added: "On the other hand, I'm sorry to say that I don't think the court did a very good job.[2] Fancy its basing such a really revolutionary decision merely on sociological data, and blatantly discarding historical and legal materials. They could have made a really good case."

[2] In *Brown* v. *Topeka*, 347 US 483 (1954), the school desegregation case.

I agree that *Brown* v. *Topeka* was a good decision and a disappointing opinion, and I think this not only from the standpoint of legal craftsmanship, which is not within my competence anyway, but from the unfortunate effects it had on Southern compliance. The court's reliance on sociological findings may have great merit, nevertheless, if it be read as acknowledging a fundamental fact—that we could not and cannot simply *will* or decree civil rights, that we must indeed confront the sociological and economic roots of discrimination. To recognize the civil rights of Negro Americans is to cause our society to quake, because racial discrimination has been at its foundation. We cannot merely decide to stop doing certain things and to stop omitting the doing of others. Discrimination was and is less a matter of will than of system, and to eradicate it requires systematic adjustments. Beyond civil rights the objective is something called integration, but integration into a society that has been and is systematically discriminatory is patently impossible; the society and its ways of conducting itself must be in some substantial measure reshaped and refurnished.

Saying this is not, however, enough, for it begs an interesting, indeed a basic, question of political theory. What kind of a "system" is a social order? The social contract theorists of the seventeenth and eighteenth centuries insisted that society was not an organism bound by and inseparable from deep historical roots. The roots themselves these theorists saw as existing only through the tolerance of the present moment. Consequently, they viewed a social order as altogether the responsibility of living men, renewed constantly by their decisions. I think they were correct. The social system is fueled and enforced moment to moment by individual actions and decisions. We cannot will that it produce other than it is contrived to produce; no more can we deny or ignore that the contrivance itself is sustained and formed by our willing.

The Negro revolt invokes society's good will, but not at a superficial, easy level. It must reach to the embedded rings and bearings of the social machine. The revolt has been in truth an antirevolution; it has not called primarily for a change of the legal order, but for changes in society in order to conform to the legal constitution and its spirit. Most impressively, it has been a revolution carried through, every step of the way, under the stimulus and protection of the legal constitution. Surely no other great social and political reform of its proportions anywhere else in the West could have claimed that quality. Moreover, the Negro revolt demands integration, and the United States is again in its history lucky, for revolutionists who wish to join society, rather than smash it, are rare.

To date, the civil-rights movement, in addition to its direct gains for Negro Southerners, has carried us to several adjustments in the federal system, adjustments which I believe increase the likelihood that state governments will continue to have an important role in American politics; it has given strong, probably decisive, impetus to the reapportionment campaign; it has caused us to deepen and widen our concepts of public responsibility for the poor and for the education of all our children and youth. During the wretched years prelude to the Civil War, much weaker pressures and much simpler problems had overwhelmed the talents and patriotism of the country's statesmen, baffled the intelligence of the public, and revealed the weakness of courts, legislatures, and executives. By contrast and unless something goes terribly wrong, the struggle for Negro equality which began at a new level during World War II will almost certainly appear to future generations as one of the truly bright chapters of accomplishment in American history.

The emergence of Negro Americans—not yet citizens in any other than a fictitious sense—from the status of wards to the privileges and duties of the self-reliant began, as all things do, gradually and almost imperceptibly. Not altogether arbitrarily, however, special acknowledgment may be given to June 25, 1941. A. Philip Randolph and the March on Washington Committee had asked President Roosevelt for protection against discriminatory employment in the federal government and the defense industries. The President sought to dissuade them from the proposed march. They persisted with their plan. The President gave in, and by Executive Order the Fair Employment Practice Committee was created.[3]

For the first time, a well-equipped demand had been made by Negro leadership (not by white persons in behalf of Negroes), had been supported by sufficient and negotiable power, and had consequently been heard and granted. Thus was established what

[3] Executive Order 8802. Superseded by Executive Order 9346, May 17, 1943.

was to become the classic formula, one not used before, and one that since 1954 has been the invariable means by which Negro gains have been made.

The wartime FEPC accomplished notable results, though the labor scarcity of the war years was undoubtedly the larger cause for some barriers falling and for heavy gains in Negro employment.[4] More importantly, the FEPC assaulted the social legitimacy of discrimination.

That assault was continued by President Truman. In late 1946 he appointed his Committee on Civil Rights. Its report of 1947 was not the usual cautious product of a presidential commission, but a candid indictment of the nation's disregard for its own legal constitution, and of the nation's refusal to take seriously the duty it had assumed to guarantee or at least defend constitutional rights. The report reasserted a position that had been abandoned seventy years earlier, that equality of rights was a national responsibility. President Truman accepted the report and henceforth by legislative proposals, by public statements, and by political daring gave it unqualified support. The national will in regard to America's oldest and cruelest problem began to be reformed.

The President's actions in 1947, at the Democratic convention of 1948 in Philadelphia, and during the 1948 campaign were either an awesome example of political courage or an almost incredible display of political canniness; perhaps they were both, but I lean toward the former view. Mr. Truman had faults, but

[4] See Louis Ruchames, *Race, Jobs and Politics* (New York: Columbia University, 1953).

his presidency was ennobled because of his stubborn conviction that a problem was something to be faced and a President's job was to make decisions. Here was a Democratic President from a border state, with many personal and political attachments to Southern politicians, facing an election which appeared likely to go against him, harassed by labor problems at home and the most desperate sorts of problems abroad, yet nevertheless deliberately choosing a position bound to antagonize his party's traditional bastion of strength and which in fact cost him the electoral votes of four Southern states. The importance of the election of 1948 can hardly be overstated. It began the amending process of the real constitution. It proposed the repeal of the South's veto power; sixteen years later the proposal was to be ratified by passage of the Civil Rights Act of 1964.

President Truman's Executive Order 9981 of July 26, 1948, stated a policy of nondiscrimination in the armed services; it was made a reality by General Matthew Ridgway's command decision in Korea, though the task of removing racial inequities within the military establishment is not yet fully done with. Strangely, scant attention has been given to this, one of the few crucially important acts in the progress of civil rights.[5] Military service is separated from normal public life, but in the years since 1950 hundreds of thousands of young men, white and Negro, Southerner and Northerner, have had an experience of integration which is hardly yet provided by any civilian institution, have

[5] See Nichols, *Breakthrough on the Color Front* (New York: Random House, 1954).

had their prejudices rearranged and their ambitions kindled.

The Supreme Court joined the presidency in making the period between World War II and 1954 one of immense but orderly change. The court's most valuable decision was the 1944 ruling in *Smith* v. *Allwright*,[6] striking down the legal foundation for the white primary. From near zero in 1944, Negro voter registration in the eleven Southern states rose to over 1,000,000 by 1952, storing up the political leverage which in the years after 1954 would be one of the powerful forces breaking the unanimity of the South's defense of white supremacy. Two decisions of 1950— *Sweatt* v. *Painter* and *McLaurin* v. *Oklahoma*—declared the rights of Negroes to attend public institutions of higher education, a right which twelve years later nearly 30,000 federal troops would defend for James Meredith at the University of Mississippi, but which by September 1954 had been peaceably accorded at thirty public colleges and universities in the old Confederacy, though by none at all in Alabama, Florida, Georgia, Mississippi, or South Carolina.

The voting and the higher education cases seemed at first to show that judicial processes could effectively engineer social reform. This effectiveness ceased when the job was far from done. An earlier leading case, *Shelley* v. *Kraemer*, was and is, nevertheless, of first-rank importance, because in removing from racially restrictive housing covenants all legal enforceability

[6] 321 US 649. For the other cases mentioned in this and the next paragraph, the citations are, in order, 339 US 629; 339 US 637; 334 US 1.

it made residential segregation slightly less impregnable and moved the Federal Housing Administration, finally, in 1949, to remove from its appraisal manual the stress on racial homogeneity in all FHA insured projects and to stop encouraging restrictive covenants, administrative practices whose profound and omnipresent consequence to urban economics and national honor will long be with us.

The record of the years 1942 to 1954 is impressive, and made more so by the frequent cases in which the Supreme Court, troubled so badly in *Screws* v. *U.S.*[7] in applying statutory protections for due process, continued to find in the constitution itself the means to protect in some measure the Negro Southerner in his ancient warfare with his local and state police and courts. During these years change occurred through the established and regular workings of executive and judicial power. Everything was done strictly according to legal norms. As those norms were applied, they were generally obeyed. Although the Deep South states—particularly Alabama, Georgia, and Louisiana —began to experiment with newly rigorous and capricious literacy tests to bar Negro voting, these were some years off from becoming effective deterrents. On the eve of *Brown* v. *Topeka,* and after a decade of more substantial progress than had occurred since Re-

[7]325 US 91 (1945). At issue was an effort by the Department of Justice to breathe life into one of the old Reconstruction statutes, through prosecution of a Georgia sheriff for a savage killing of a Negro prisoner. Four differing opinions were written by the Justices, in no one of which did a majority concur.

construction, one could say and believe that the American system of orderly change was working well.

It stopped working in 1954. First, Southern reactions to *Brown* v. *Topeka* had been, on the whole, mild. They were not to remain so. By the fall of the year, as election campaigns heated, and under the leadership of Governor Talmadge and Governor-elect Griffin of Georgia, Senator Byrd of Virginia, and outgoing Governor Byrnes of South Carolina, the South was in full defiance. The rebellion, and it was that, would last throughout most of the South for the next five years, and in the deepest recesses of the South for longer. For the second time within a century, the South offered combat to federal authority, combat this time not of arms but of evasion, harassment, and blatant nonobedience. The result was to bear witness to the danger of winning wars and neglecting to win the peace that follows. For the Civil War had been about slavery, about Southern political preeminence within the Union, about what would happen to the West. The South lost the war and it lost the West. But segregation was allowed to succeed slavery, and the political power, if not preeminence, of the South was rebuilt and became the moat of Southern separatism.

It is difficult to convey to persons who did not live in the South during those years a feeling of how it was. The difficulty would be greater had not all the country experienced the ravages of McCarthyism. Imagine the emotional and political atmosphere of the McCarthy days intensified many times and compressed within a single region, and the South of the late 1950's may be suggested. The rebellion reached its climax in late 1958 when Virginia, historic leader of the South, closed the schools of Norfolk, Charlottesville, and Warren County, and Arkansas did likewise in Little Rock. If one likes Civil War analogies, this was Gettysburg, the South's invasion of a field which was an essential part of the American union; not this time a geographic field but a cultural one: the public-school system. Governor Almond's capitulation on January 28, 1959, and the prompt reopening of the Virginia schools, was the retreat from Gettysburg. Like that earlier one, it was not pursued.

The orderly change of 1941–54 had manifested the strength of the constitution. The rebellion after 1954 showed how necessary to the working of a constitution is the habit of obedience. The South stopped obeying, and the constitution thereafter had throughout the South only permissive status. Not only did the South successfully defy *Brown* v. *Topeka,* but virtually all other change stopped as well. A firm bar was thrown across college and university campuses. Prior to 1955 the desegregation of colleges and universities had been uneventful and seemingly was gathering momentum; for the next five years almost no advance was made, and ahead lay the bitter controversies of the universities of Alabama (twice), Georgia, and Mississippi. Voting registration by Negroes slowed abruptly. Across the eleven states, the number of Negro voters increased about 400,000 between 1952 and 1960, but this represented an increase of only 2 percent (from 20 percent to 22 percent) in the number of eligible Negroes registered, and, moreover, the increase was confined almost entirely to urban centers outside the Deep South. In other areas, too, resistance hardened and some old gains were reversed; biracial meetings of any kind, for example, became more rare and the hiring of Negro police practically ceased.

Attributing blame to individuals is a poor sport, but three men are worthy of remark, because not only did much depend on them but each was politically free to have given a different kind of leadership. Senator Harry F. Byrd of Virginia has never attracted the condemnation given to a Governor Barnett or a Governor Wallace, but quite likely his influence was greater. Mastermind of Virginia's doctrine and policy of "massive resistance" and principal promoter of the Southern Manifesto of March 1956, he was as responsible as any single individual for the organization of the Southern rebellion.

No more politically pressed was Governor Orval Faubus of Arkansas, who, to general surprise, followed the earlier and less conspicuous example of Governor Shivers of Texas and put state power in direct conflict with federal authority.

Hardest of all to comprehend was Dwight D. Eisenhower's conception of the American presidency. The equivocation and ambiguities of his press conference of September 5, 1956, following Governor Shivers defiance at Mansfield, Texas, can hardly be read today without rueful realization that Governor Faubus had much to rely on in his more spectacular defiance of the following year. The President's reaction to the Southern Manifesto was that of a man seemingly uninformed as to events and their meaning.

In 1957 he scuttled his own administration's proposal to grant the attorney general authority to bring school desegregation suits in the name of the United States. A few weeks later he did what could not be avoided and ordered troops to Little Rock. But this was hardly decisive leadership; it was the ugly outcome of a lack of leadership. The Eisenhower administration ended its term brilliantly in the New Orleans school crisis of 1960–61, when new men in the Department of Justice forged the legal concept of defending the integrity of the federal courts. To calculate, however, the violence done to the public peace by the President's six-year-long policy of neutrality would be neither easy nor unfair.

Before the void in federal leadership could be filled, a new force to oppose the rebellion arose, and in the South itself. By 1960 there were already holes in the Southern fortress, but ones of little effect. In the school year 1959–60, only 4200 Negro children were in classrooms with whites throughout the region, and of these three-fourths were in West Texas, and a big portion of the small remainder in predominantly Negro schools in Miami. No school desegregation at all had occurred in South Carolina, Georgia, Alabama, Louisiana, or Mississippi. The great cities of East Texas—Houston, Dallas, Fort Worth—were as yet unaffected; so were Memphis, Chattanooga, Richmond, and all of Florida except Miami. In three North Carolina cities (Charlotte, Greensboro, and Winston-Salem) the number of Negro children in classes with whites had moved from eleven in 1957–58, the first year, to a grand total of thirteen in 1959–60.

The need was for leadership to impel the South to move. It could have come from Congress or the President; it did not. Beginning in February 1960, it did come from Negro youth. They, by their sit-ins, led the white South to do something which it had never before in history done. In community after community—more than eighty by the end of 1960—lunch-counters were desegregated; never before, and this is a startling fact, had the South yielded racial restrictions without federal coercion. But more than this, the students galvanized civil-rights adherents into a movement, forced white Southerners to confront at least some of their responsibilities, put a whole region astir intellectually and emotionally, and captured the attention and admiration of public opinion in the North and West. The swamp at last was being bridged, and Americans were finally being guided from its moral and political morass.

Under the direction of President Truman, the republic had begun to accept its constitution, to give it respect and force. By 1954 the South had accepted all that its political rulers saw fit to allow. In the absence of presidential purpose, and with too few interested congressmen to match the Southerners, Southern rebellion was able to defeat or, at the least, to cripple severely federal authority. The student movement restored direction. Its promise was that the republic would accept the constitution it had given itself.

What has happened is, I think, a rare occurrence in the history of governments. Law usually is fitted to social reality, legal norms are made to conform to the real constitution. That was what had occurred during the years when segregation was being fastened on the South and given legal license. Now we were to see a strange thing. We were to witness the real constitution bent to the requirements of the legal constitution.

According to C. Vann Woodward,[8] during the Civil War the North first committed itself to the cause of union, then gradually adopted emancipation as a war and Reconstruction aim, and then acknowledged, but only with lip service and not enduringly, the goal of equality for Negroes. Similarly, we might say that in the great contest brought on by the South's post-1954 rebellion, the republic's interest was first of all primarily only law and order and the acknowledgment, however nominal, of federal supremacy. We have moved in thought and will if not in full practice to accept as a second objective the one at which the post-Civil War generation balked: political equality. We face beyond it, however, our own third stage, and whether we shall meet and overcome it is far from clear; no more clear than was the determination of the men of the 1860's to make real the promises of equality.

I refer to what we call "integration" or, if one prefers, a true equalization of opportunity. If constitutional norms are now being respected and the veto power of the South is now fading, the rule and privilege of the white race is still a reality, and the actual constitution of this republic still contains its aged element of dangerous instability. If we should ask our-

[8] *The Burden of Southern History* (Baton Rouge, La.: Louisiana State University Press, 1960).

selves now, after a decade and more of struggle, who has directly benefitted from it all, the candid answer would be, I think, only the Southerner—only the Negro Southerner with his new rights and the white Southerner with his new freedom from his ancient calling as the oppressor of his neighbor. Negroes of the North have profited little in a direct way and, for that matter, their brothers in the South are little if any better off except in the perquisites of dignity. These facts are becoming widely known; what waits answer is whether we shall master them.

There is one bright difference between our times and those of Reconstruction. Preservation of the union, antislavery, equality—these were then the aims of one group of effective persons only: Northern whites. Law and order, equality, and integration are the aims of a muscular Negro movement North and South, of many and influential Northern whites, and of a large and growing minority of white Southerners who accept the first two of the aims and more of the third than is commonly supposed. We are a closer nation now.

This democracy was capable of emancipating slaves, but not of making citizens of them; perhaps no democracy could have. So though we who are white do right to feel sorrow for the Negroes' historic injustices, in truth their rights could not be granted until they learned to demand them; or, in other words, not until Negroes began to act like citizens.

Emancipation had, in a sense, come too easily. Although many Negroes fought bravely and died in the Civil War, it remained essentially a white man's fight, and emancipation was his gift. What he gave he could take back, and did, in substance if not in law. The freedom being secured in the 1960's is not a gift, but a victory.

Today, white persons are amazed by the rapidity and extent of change. Negroes despair over the slow progress. This difference of view flows from what is the essence of the Negro revolt. That essence is a demand that white people see and value the Negro as he sees and values himself or, in still too many cases, as he wishes to see and value himself. The Negro finds that there has been little progress because his demand is that he be valued *now* as a person of worth and that he be able truly to see himself *now* as someone of value.

The Negro revolt is a drive toward integration. It is a search also by Negroes for a new and quickened sense of identity. There is some conflict between a desire to integrate with white society and a desire to establish a resolute identity, and the conflict produces a tension throughout the Negro community.

This same Negro revolt has led the *pars valentior*—the prevailing part—of American democracy toward a painful revaluation of itself and its institutions. White America has been shaken by the Negro search for integration and identity, and its own self-assurance has been deeply wounded. Perhaps the wisest discovery of James Baldwin was that no American, Negro or white, has a given identity, that we have always been and are now a people in search of ourselves.[9] In the tension of these times, it may be that all America will find a clearer self-knowledge.

[9] *Nobody Knows My Name* (New York: Dial Press, 1961), p. 137.

II

★ ★ ★ ★ ★

Second Reconstruction

"LET US BEGIN," said Ulrich Phillips as he set out on his story of *Life and Labor in the Old South*,[1] "by discussing the weather, for that has been the chief agency in making the South distinctive." W. J. Cash noted at the opening of his great book[2] that "there exists among us by ordinary—both North and South—a profound conviction that the South is another land, sharply differentiated from the rest of the American nation, and exhibiting within itself a remarkable homogeneity."

This is how it has been with the South. A region set itself apart and grew together into a likeness that conquers immense internal differences of history, land, dialect, and even climate. The South beguiles and maddens those who have loved her most intensely. She fascinates those who stridently rage against her. The South is drawing to its close as a discrete political power. Its civilization also is ending, or, rather, is headed toward sameness with all America. No writer

[1] Boston: Little, Brown, 1929.
[2] *The Mind of the South* (New York: Alfred A. Knopf, 1941).

of a decade or so hence will need to explore the mind
of the South, as Cash did, for it is about to become
as mindless as New England or the mid-West and in
the near future will have finally found its rest in the
American union. One says this with sorrow. Gross as
have been her sins and uncouth as have been many
of her ways, the South inspired her sons and daugh-
ters, even her suffering black ones, to love her. What
other region did that, and in doing it gave dimension
and stamina to human spirits?

The white South has liked to imagine its lineage
to be in old England and its style of thought to come
from there and classical Greece and Rome. The South
has in fact owed most of its culture to Africa and
New England: to Africa which gave it so many of its
hands and so much of its style, and to New England
which gave it its soul. Puritanism was an unlikely
fruit to transplant into the South, but somehow it took
root and spread like a creeper vine. In all the austere
annals of Puritanism, nowhere has the cult of the
moral athlete flourished as it has in the South. But
with a difference. The Southern Puritan—and that
label applies to nearly all the population—by and large,
and ordinarily, expects to lose. Generally speaking,
he has known all along that he will probably, when
his crucial test comes, lose the battle between good
and evil. And so he has differed from his fellow Americans in two important particulars: his conscience has
hurt him mercilessly, and he has been compassionate
about human shortcomings. Morality had a way of
leading the white Southerner sooner or later to do
something about the Negro, something he wouldn't do;

so he would fail, and grow weary in self-knowledge. Self-respect would sooner or later lead the Negro Southerner to steps he would not take; and so he would fail, and grow sad. Civil rights is psychotherapy for the South; the physician's price is, however, high: never another Faulkner, never another glorious outpouring of sorrow songs and mighty spirituals.

Will the psychotherapy extend also to removing from the South what has been its one outstanding virtue, its compassion for individual frailty? This has been the root, probably, of the characteristically theological cast of Southern thought: of seeing all lives as under the judgment of God and of knowing, therefore, with certainty the transience of all works of men. The South has largely kept this knowledge to itself, though spread about over the country it might have thinned American presumption. A Southerner doubting the permanence of anything may as well doubt also the permanence of his own doubting. That is, at least, the safer course, and from it comes a suspicion that as the vice of the South dies, so too will its virtue. If by some chance it does not, then a South which has no longer a dark mind to be explored may yet have a thought to give, a thought nourished and lighted by its own special history of tribulation, a thought that dwells on and takes a humbling measure of the vicissitudes that befall all human striving.

Lillian Smith began her classic with these words: "Even its children knew that the South was in trouble. No one had to tell them; no words said aloud, . . . This haunted childhood belongs to every Southerner of any age. We ran away from it but we came back like a hurt animal to its wound, or a murdererer to the scene of his sin. The human heart dares not stay away too long from that which hurts it most. . . . We who were born in the South called this mesh of feeling and memory 'loyalty.' We thought of it sometimes as 'love.' We identified with the South's trouble as if we, individually, were responsible for all of it. . . . It is a strange thing, this umbilical cord uncut. . . . when we are threatened with change, suddenly it draws the whole white South together."[3]

The young Negro author, Ronald V. Fair, in his brilliant novel *Many Thousands Gone*,[4] sensed this drawing together. In the Mississippi of his story, "the vulgar, illiterate sheriff had outwitted the entire United States government because all the time he had known something they didn't know. He knew he was at war with the Yankee forces; he knew he was fighting the same war his great-grandfather fought." There is another war also, and Ralph Ellison told of it: "He was an odd old guy, my grandfather, and I am told I take after him. It was he who caused the trouble. On his deathbed he called my father to him and said, 'Son, after I'm gone, I want you to keep up the good fight. I never told you, but our life is a war and I have been a traitor all my born days, a spy in the enemy's country ever since I give up my gun back in the Reconstruction. Live with your head in the lion's mouth. I want you to overcome 'em with yeses, undermine 'em with grins, agree 'em to death and destruction, let

[3] *Killers of the Dream*, revised edition (New York: Norton, 1961).
[4] New York: Harcourt, Brace and World, 1965.

'em swóller you till they vomit or bust wide open!' "[5]

Warfare of Southerner and Yankee, white and Negro, warfare unceasing, vigilance always required, vigilance the very watchword of living, even when seeming most relaxed or indolent, because always the opponent is near. It is a curious quality, this vigilance, one that has often baffled the outsider. For Southerners themselves, it has been for many a tension that exhausted them before their time, for others a coiled spring that has kept them ahead. At the core of it always has been the Negro, for the Yankee is only an interloper and the Negro is his own keenest adversary.

Thus, Southern society from Virginia to Texas was organized around the principle that Negroes must not be permitted equality with the white race in any area or in any form. This became the highest public value, and to support it the ideology of white supremacy was elaborated and made well-nigh sacred. Politics became of central importance, for the values and the philosophy were public—belonged to the public—and therefore required a common defense. Politicians consequently were seen, typically, not only or even most importantly as the public's servants, but as the sentries and guardians and sometimes the field marshals and, in whatever aspect, as somehow partaking of a priestly function, for the public philosophy had become a civil religion. At home the officeholders were the ever-vigilant patrons and protectors; sent off to Washington, they were ministers plenipotentiary.

One can be deeply attached to the South and still find almost no tolerance for its typical politician

[5] *Invisible Man* (New York: Random House, 1953).

or its structure of political power. At every crisis of Southern history the region's statesmen have led the South wrongly—most conspicuously in 1860 and after May 17, 1954. No irresistible popular demand drove Senator Byrd, Governor Faubus, or even Governor Byrnes in his course, and the injury done by the men of the late 1950's was not just to Negroes nor just to national unity, but to the region they claimed to champion.

One can, moreover, acknowledge the usefulness of conservative checks and still find no ground to respect the generality of Southern congressmen, for their conservatism has seldom been more than a tawdry blend of racism and vested interests. One can, in short, correctly view politics as the most glaring of Southern failures, and its politicians as the expectable fruit of a political system built piece by piece on a foundation of racial fear.

Nor can the generations of the South's politicians validly take to themselves much credit for preserving white supremacy as long as they did. The dirty work was done by the men who stayed at home in state and local offices, and it was done dirtily. The congressmen had little to defend during the long years of national noninterest between the 1870's and the 1930's. They did hold off congressional action for a quarter century after the New Deal took office, though in not all of those years was there genuine threat.

The system was an almost perfect contrivance for insuring irresponsibility on everyone's part; in this as well as in its basic mechanism it was remarkably like twentieth-century despotisms. The essential conditions were. the removal of the vast Negro minority from political life and the elimination of party competition, thus insulating regional politics from unwanted outside influences. Once having done these things, the prime, the overriding, necessity was to keep them done. Defense against the alien and internal security were the only truly important purposes, and political contest was dominated by claims of victory and counterclaims of greater prowess, by accusations and counteraccusations of disloyalty. The individual citizen had little to do with this; he found one reason or another for voting as he did, but he knew that there was little loss or gain either way. This same system, which made his leaders neglect his interests, made him impotent. Of all American voters, he was assuredly the most easily led.

His wrath, on the other hand, could be great. Yet nothing is more clear in all the history of the South than his willingness to accept federal authority when clearly made evident. The populace did not impel the South to secession nor, in the 1950's, to defiance. It was led into the crisis of the 1950's and 1960's, and the best that can be said for the men who led is that, in revulsion against the dreary sordidness of their accustomed roles, they sought the imagined cleanliness of battle.

And yet—and this is part of the eternal, the profound, call of the South—to every statement made in the preceding two paragraphs, paragraphs that formulate a type in terms long familiar, any informed student can cite rebutting evidence, and weighty evidence at that. The whole is true, as true as a simple portrait of a society of people can ever be. All of the parts are misleading. It is so easy to encapsulate the South: almost any full-throated denunciation will do; so too will many tender tales. But the South has to be lived to be known, and the living is never quite like the formula. Time and again one can sit in a room where Negro Southerners talk with friends, white or Negro, from the North, and hear sometime, some inevitable time, late in the conversation, one of the former draw back from the catharsis of regional ridicule and criticism and hesitantly explain, "No, it's not just that way—." One talks with the white youths who came down from the North for the Mississippi summer of 1964, and one hears of newly felt appreciation, of an awareness of some vague charm, of an unexpected discovery of human strength. One goes to a White House reception for civil-rights people, and on the President's table of hors d'oeuvres is a platter of barbecued ribs, with Southern accents buzzing hungrily around, and suddenly there is a fraternity of white and black that for the moment makes every Northern white man and every Northern Negro too long gone an outsider. Such things are the South's patrimony of mystery, and somehow that mystery is as much its essence as its sin.

The sin was, and is, the main thing. The greatest of all the sinning was not that white men killed and raped and cheated Negroes, nor even that white men induced Negroes to kill and rape and cheat themselves. The mortal sin was that white men united to defend this as a right, as a way of life, and did so in the name of their God. No charm, no mystery, no rapturous appeal could excuse this. It had to be, and has to be, destroyed.

The first serious modern challenge came with the antilynching and poll tax bills of the late 1930's, and Southern senators were pressed into a six-week long filibuster in 1937–38 in order to kill the antilynching bill; it was not merely coincidental that from then on the Southern congressional support that had helped make the New Deal reforms possible began to fade off, nor that from then until the Kennedy administration there occurred a widespread stoppage of economic and social reform by legislation. The coalition of Southern Democrats and so-called conservative Republicans ruled Congress, and each was needed by the other. We had the paradox, which some political scientists began to assume was the norm, of congressional control by conservative forces while the presidents, whether Democratic or Republican, were responsive to big city majorities. The civil-rights enactments of 1957, 1960, 1964, and 1965 were prelude to the remarkable outpouring of legislation in the 1964 and 1965 sessions.

Congress had again become free. During the intervening years it had been hardly a governing body. The constitution is hinged on a Congress of force and dignity. It has not always been such, and in the years before 1961 the record of Congress is puzzling to appraise. It was chiefly absorbed in foreign policy and national defense, in investigations, and in criticizing and checking executive actions; there was only a

limited fulfillment of legislative initiative. Foreign relations and defense were central, and Congress, generally speaking, supported and reinforced the policies
of the presidents; it is not clear that a legislature can
responsibly act otherwise in this field, and the Congress of the 1940's and 1950's is, therefore, entitled to
some portion of history's respect. I can here only
assert, not argue, this conclusion, just as I can only
state my belief that congressional preoccupation during this era with investigations was unsavory, and its
essential role of criticizing and checking the executive
was excessively and badly performed. As a delibera-
tive body, conceiving or perfecting legislation and
policy, the chief contributions of these Congresses
came at those few times when a conservative majority
could be assembled for innovation rather than mere
obstruction, and the results, typified by the Taft-
Hartley Act or the Internal Security Act of 1950, indicate the color of the period's conservatism. Senator
Taft had the affection of his fellow conservatives, but
he almost alone among them had an interest in devis-
ing a conservative strategy toward economic and
social needs and issues.

The negativistic conservative congressmen of
those years made their force almost unmoveable by
use of the structure and processes of Congress. In doing so, they reduced the stature of Congress and seriously imperiled the separation of powers. Governments
must govern, and the inevitable consequence of congressional negativism was the enhancement of presidential and judicial leadership. There is in the constitution itself enough protection for congressional auton-

omy. To bolster constitutional authority with the use of Senate Rule 22[6] and the House Rules Committee, to refuse to take any responsibility for redistricting within the states or for flagrant violations of the Fifteenth Amendment, to enthrone committee chairmen, and to choose them religiously by seniority—to do these things were not the marks of a vigorous and independent legislature but of one determined on its own diminution. Congress was unconcernedly watching itself become progressively less and less a representative body, and at the same time was making itself almost incapable of exercising governing authority and power. If the separation of powers thrives in this republic, it will be only because the Supreme Court by its decisions in and following *Baker* v. *Carr*[7] came to the legislature's rescue, and because the Negro revolt loosened the grip of negativism.

By 1965 the Southern senatorial caucus was down to nineteen participants, many of whom were elderly and some of the younger of whom were noticeably restive. The Tennessee senators had not for years sat with it, nor did one of the Texas senators. Two members of the caucus—from South Carolina and Texas— were Republicans, implying by their presence a growing threat to the tenure of all others, for Republicanism was having a steady growth in the region. Border state senators were no longer the allies they had been

[6] The rule, now somewhat modified, protecting filibusters.
[7] 369 US 186, 1962. This was the great decision establishing the principle that the federal courts could examine the fairness and test the constitutionality of legislative representation in the states.

during the 1930's and 1940's, and the men from the mountain states had given up trading with the South. In the House, twenty-two representatives from the South voted for the Voting Rights act of 1965.[8]

The veto power of the South has been ended, and with its demise American government had new strength to work well. Political science has not yet agreed on its basic findings, but R. M. MacIver's rule of "single alignment"[9] may well be a near invariable criterion of governmental stability. The political issues on which men choose sides must either fall along a single division, whether it be economic, religious, constitutional, or other, or else the government cannot effectively function. The issues of the South and of white supremacy were paralyzing confusions in the political order. They intruded time after time into efforts to resolve and move ahead on other and more rational questions.

We have tended not to want to face these sectional and racial issues directly. We have wanted to

[8] In 1957 one Southern representative—a Republican from Tennessee—voted for the civil rights act of that year. The Act of 1960 was voted for by one representative from Florida, two—both Republican—from Tennessee, and six representatives from Texas: total, nine. The Act of 1964 had one representative from Florida voting for it, one from Georgia, two from Tennessee (both Democrats; all three of the state's Republicans now were opposed), and four from Texas: total, eight. The 1965 act was supported by six members from Florida, two from Georgia, two from Louisiana, four from Tennessee, and eight from Texas.

[9] *The Modern State* (New York: Oxford University Press, 1947), pp. 406–16.

say that education, economic growth, unionism, or population dispersal would in time solve them. We shirked from recognizing that the issues were issues of power. Ronald Fair's Mississippi sheriff outsmarts the federal government because he knows this, and the government does not. Fair's novel closed with the Negroes of the sheriff's county wresting power away from the sheriff, while the federal marshals who had been sent to protect them remained his helpless prisoners; the Negroes then unlocked the doors, and set their emancipators free. The symbolism is perfect.

The Southern rebellion is ended. What now of the South?

In a recent number of the *Southern Economic Journal*, one writer concluded:

. . . the region cannot as yet boast of a single outstanding institution [of higher education] on the national scene. It has a fair share of good universities, but perhaps more than its share of poor ones. The scene would be little altered if we had concentrated on liberal arts colleges.

To this uncharitable view, a gracious gentleman and discussant from Indiana demurred, saying:

. . . we could carve out a region that would consist of the Dakotas, Montana, Wyoming, Idaho, Colorado, Nevada, Nebraska, Kansas, Arizona, and New Mexico and . . . in this region we would find very few institutions like Duke, Emory, North Carolina, Texas, Tulane, Vanderbilt, or Virginia.

This of course doesn't prove a thing other than that regional comparisons surely are interesting.[10]

The difference, of course, is that the eleven contiguous Western states do not think of themselves as a single region, and consequently no one else does. The South still sees itself as common region. It may be well that this is so.

It may be well, because the South has experienced battle this last decade and perhaps has grown in wisdom and energy from it. In one aspect the South's history since 1954 is a history of sorrow. In another aspect, it is not, it is a history of honor, for if one believes that all life is struggle, that the contest between liberty and tyranny is never ceasing, that men can have no higher calling than to defend liberty against tyranny, if one believes this then he may take note that in the South of this republic men fought well and they won. The Southerner can know now, because he has experienced it, how easy it is to adopt despotism. For a space of years he endured an orthodoxy of opinion, a curtailment of dissent, and a regimentation of political life that were very close to being totalitarian. Subverted by demagogues and mob rule, he fought his way free.

He was able to do it because a new leadership appeared and continues. The same Negroes who had given the region, all through its history, its communal bond, now leagued with whites who in the 1950's

[10]Allan M. Cartter, "Qualitative Aspects of Southern University Education," *The Southern Economic Journal*, July 1965 Supplement, p. 63. Comment by Howard G. Scholler, *op. cit.*, p. 72.

could fight only defensive actions, are the force of momentum over most of the region.

The strength of this new Negro leadership lay in its stubborn naiveté, in its blindness to what all the rest of Southern society, including its white liberals, knew to be a fact and to what the non-South also generally accepted as a fact. Segregation and the lesser forms of discrimination were a condition of life in America, a resultant of history woven into the social fabric and susceptible of only gradual melioration. This was a fact, which all of America, more or less, understood—except the new Negro leadership, which denied it. Segregation was not, in their eyes, a condition. It was a policy and, as such, could be changed abruptly. And this is what the Negro leaders taught the rest of us. They made us acknowledge that America present—and not just America past—was responsible and that segregation and discrimination were enforced by concerted and active policy.

This teaching was a tremendous gift to American vitality, because once we recognized that segregation was not a condition of life but a policy adopted anew each day, once we could convict ourselves of responsibility, we could act. The invigoration carried further, to other problems that had seemed to be ingrained conditions of American life, such as inequitable representation, poverty, the Catholic Church's position on birth control, and the specious church-state controversy that had frustrated federal aid to education. In one field after another, we began to shake off the despotism of institutional rigidity, and the South was the spawning ground of the new vitality.

The contest in the South against nativist despotism had begun even before 1954. The South's early enthusiasm for the New Deal never altogether died out and in the late 1940's showed signs of reviving. Men such as Scott of North Carolina, Arnall of Georgia, Folsom of Alabama, McMath of Arkansas, and Browning of Tennessee won election as governors. Kefauver went to the Senate in 1948 from Tennessee, and there joined Pepper of Florida and Hill and Sparkman of Alabama, staunch New Dealers, as was, much of the way, Johnston of South Carolina; in a short while and for a short while, Graham of North Carolina would be with them. Even in Virginia the liberal tide almost succeeded. Virginians went to bed on election night in August 1949 believing that Francis Pickens Miller had broken the Byrd machine and had been chosen governor, only to have late returns go against him.

Georgia in 1946 ballotted for a successor to Ellis Arnall. The majority of the popular vote went to James Carmichael, pledged to continue the reform administration of Arnall, but Eugene Talmadge was the winner through Georgia's almost inexpressibly vicious system of county unit votes. During the next several years, in state after state, a reversal somewhat like the Georgia election of 1946 was to occur. The 1950 defeats of Frank Graham in North Carolina and of Claude Pepper by George Smathers in Florida set a tone of racist viciousness that was frightening.

Calvin Kytle, acting director of the U.S. Community Relations Service,[11] wrote in *Harper's Maga-*

[11] Resigned December 1965.

zine (September 1948) an article titled "A Long Dark Night for Georgia," a dismal, despondent view of the state's future following Herman Talmadge's political advent. The predictions seemed exaggeratedly pessimistic. Recently, I reread the article, and though it has proved to be erroneous in some of its detailed predictions, its only serious fault was its underestimation of the degradation that Georgia—and for that matter the South generally—would reach during the next decade.

Only in Tennessee did the men who came forward in the late 1940's survive in politics, and this may have had considerable to do with the fact that only the Tennessee state government never mouthed massive resistance or wholeheartedly practiced it.

If I have talked here of men it is because I know of no other way to discuss Southern politics. If I have talked of politics, it is because I know of no other way to talk of the South. The life of the region has centered around politics with unusual closeness. The wholesome side of this concentration is that ideas of public service have been deeply rooted and encouraged. The obverse has been a curious but typically prevalent blend of intense citizenry interest in politics combined with apathetic irresponsibility.

Given the ideological character of the region's politics, these qualities are not paradoxical. The South furnishes an instructive example of the moral and social ravages of a political order based on ideology. In the South's particular case this took the form of a one-party system, because party conflict was too risky of ideological purity to be permitted. With no second party to identify with, dissent had no efficient outlet. There were no regular forums of opposition or even criticism, and the factions into which the party split were typically unstable in their allegiances and trivial in their differences. Politics was a spectator sport of the most engrossing kind; it was also a means for obtaining special favors. But the man without a special interest to defend or enhance could seldom find either institutional or customary means for influencing public policy.

It seems safe to say that this irresponsibility, which made it possible for its politicians to stampede the region into massive resistance, is passing, along with dominance of politics by the ideology of white supremacy. The sizeable and growing Negro vote, the increase of Republicanism, and reapportionment, together with such structural changes as population shifts and industrial acceleration of which they are in part reflections, mark the passing of the Southern political tradition. As the Midwest's politics differs from New England's, as New York's differs from California's, so in the years ahead Southern politics may differ from that of other sections. But for not much longer will its differences be so great as to represent, as they have in the past, a system of different quality. The South is a land whose people not many years past were debilitated by disease; indeed, very possibly the cruelest problem of the region as recently as fifty years ago was bad health. One commentator has illustrated the progress of public health by noting that in Florida today cirrhosis of the liver kills more persons than hookworm, malaria, and pellagra combined.[12] All over the country people have died and still die of cirrhosis of the liver; only in the South did they, in notable numbers, die of hookworm, pellagra, and malaria. Only in the South were certain political diseases virulent; with their passing, the South integrates itself into the common political weal and woe of all Americans.

Politics is, or should be, the means whereby people living within a corporate society settle their issues and distribute social benefits. The traditional South used politics only incidentally for these natural purposes. The central issue of the South was race, and it tormented and violated the Southern peace from one generation to another. Yet the South was so organized that this issue could not be resolved through political processes. Politics was wrenched from its natural purpose and made to serve as a system of conventions expressly maintained to prevent any solution of the racial issue. In such a topsy-turvy political order the inevitable result was that the South languished in poverty and backwardness, because only rarely and incidentally could its political machinery be turned around to face the economic and educational problems of the region.

Southern separatism has been a primary problem throughout the republic's history. It is of great moment, therefore, to observe its ending. The second Reconstruction is working—working well enough so that we may without being guilty of fantasy wonder

[12] Thomas D. Clark, *The Emerging South* (New York: Oxford University Press, 1961), p. 39.

whether we are headed into an era of state rights, though not in the meaning of past controversy. Now that they are in process of being reconstituted on a democratic basis, state governments will be instruments of power conveniently closer to the people than to Washington. They can be reasonably expected to attract the ambitious and the talented. To a country already predisposed to decentralized policy-making and administration, state governments may perform a steadily growing share of the governmental task.

One of the grounds of assurance that the second Reconstruction will work is the steady rise in Negro officeholding. That was, of course, also a salient feature of the first Reconstruction, and when federal power left the South it proved only a frail barrier to a resurgence of white control. Negroes today, however, are winning office not because whites are disfranchised but because they are outvoted, or because redistricting has created ethnic constituencies, or because a necessary fraction of white support has been bargained for; in short, they are winning through the usual methods of American politics. Furthermore, no one can reasonably anticipate that there will be a reversal of federal policies, as there was after 1876.

I stress this because the entrance of Negroes into responsible participation in politics seems to me the primary condition of racial peace and practicable integration. Negroes need to see the political process as something that can be made to work to their advantage. In the long run, only political representatives can effectively translate Negro wants and opinions into responses of public policy; the politician is the natural successor of the demonstrator and of the civil-rights lawyer. Precisely because the United States needs to solve the problem of disadvantaged people, society needs the Negro officeholder and political organizer.

The South's traditional elevation of politics accentuates the need. Given this tradition, there is no realistic hope for Southern communities at peace with themselves unless Negroes have unfettered political opportunity and accept it.

There lie ahead for the South—and, therefore, for the nation as a whole—difficulties of serious dimension and questions as yet unanswerable. Some of these have to do with economics, some with education. I am here concerned with those political conditions which either foster a social order within which economic and educational problems can be realistically defined and treated or else an order incapable, as the South for so long has been, of functioning for the general welfare because of ideological commitments. Several such conditions in particular have a threatening countenance.

The rural Black Belt, arching from southern Virginia to east Texas, was once the richest area of the South, perhaps of the whole nation. The wealth of this cotton empire prior to the Civil War naturally attracted to it political hegemony. Today, the Black Belt is poor, its people—both white and black—have been leaving since World War I, and its educational indices are shockingly low; yet it retained political dominance of the whole region until *Baker* v. *Carr* promised an end to institutionalized cheating. The sad prospect is, however, that it will foul the regional and national conscience for some time to come; neither industrialization nor educational reform can be prudently anticipated. More likely, the Black Belt will continue for years to come to exhibit broad and deep traces of its single-minded obsession with race and its tolerance of brutality and meanness.

There are, nevertheless, reasons for hope, one a possibility and the other a fact. The former lies in the chance that if the Negroes of the rural Black belt will now vote in numbers, as they are enabled to do by the Voting Rights Act, they may impart civility and toleration to the area. The other reason takes us back again to the role of ideology. One Southern state after another has let slip the active defense of white supremacy. These state governments do little or nothing to aid civil rights or assist the welfare of Negroes, but they are no longer powerful, ever-ready engines of oppression; they have been neutralized. The Black Belt counties can no longer in most states work their policies in the sureness of succor by their state governments; even in Alabama and Mississippi they cannot invariably invoke state power to do their will. The political theory and practice of the South has been a composite of the doctrine of white supremacy, a theory of politics which regarded the defense of white supremacy as the primary obligation of all officeholders, and the institutionalized convention of rural dominance. When faithfully adhered to, as they always had been in times of regional stress, these precepts had insured a closed society. As this old political theory is relinquished, as rural dominance ends and the state power no longer serves white supremacy above all else, the closed societies of the rural South will open. And as they do, the freedom of the Black Belt to be a law to itself will be challenged.

The second threatening condition grows in the soil of the Black Belt, but not only there. If the outlawry of the Black Belt can hardly get worse, here we confront something which as yet is only a nuisance and may never become much more, yet could with little surprise become a problem of serious magnitude. The issue is, what will become of the Republican Party in the South?

For years after 1954 the Citizens Council and other segregationists almost pathetically looked for Northern and Western allies and never found them. Then in 1964, there they were. With great joy a band of the most virile segregationists set about making the state Republican parties their political homes. In some states, such as Alabama, Louisiana, and Mississippi, they found cordial hosts; in other states, such as Georgia and Tennessee, they had to displace the proprietors, and new Republicans drove out old Republicans.

I do not know what course the Republican Party will take. There are several possible turnings. What would be tragic would be a course of development by which racist politics in the South, now that its one-party stronghold is decaying, would find a new institutional form. It would be ironic, too, if the Republican Party began to develop a distinct Southern wing. Democrats might get wry satisfaction, but the country has not benefited from the existence of a Southern wing

within the Democratic Party. Now that signs point to
its termination there is no pleasure in the prospect of
the Republicans taking up that burden. The Democratic Party, with its big city, labor, and intellectual
supporters, has had a hard enough time containing
Southern racism. The Republican Party without such
balances, and with strong nativist and rightist tendencies within it already, would have a difficult time
indeed.

With the movement of more and more Negroes
into the Southern electorate, a key question will be
the political direction taken by lower-income whites.
Will they continue to vote their racial prejudice, even
if to do so means voting Republican? Will they seek
for the leadership of demagogues of the pattern of
Bilbo and the later Tom Watson—demagoguery that
combines racism and economic welfarism? Will they
follow demagogues such as Folsom of Alabama or the
Longs of Louisiana, who muted racism while cham-
pioning underdogs against economic royalists? Will
they continue, as they have in more recent years, to
follow demagogues of the pattern of Eugene and Herman Talmadge and Ross Barnett, racists who are also
defenders of wealth and vested interests. Will they,
now that old battles are lost, join their voting strength
in at least parts of the South with that of Negroes,
constituting thereby an immense Southern force in
support of the welfare state? Will they cease to vote
as a bloc, as they have always tended to do, and vote
instead on an urban-rural division? These are im-
mensely important questions not only to the South
but to the nation as a whole.

Finally, the ominous question directly ahead for

the South is the kind of new racial relations it will have. The old pattern is being discarded, and the new is not yet fashioned. This generation of adults will make decisions that will endure for years to come as to the kind of society we shall have in this land. The really key decisions will not be made by presidents, Congress, or civil-rights leaders, but by millions of homeowners, churchgoers, parents of school children, trade unionists. They will choose whether they want an open society (and today that can only mean an integrated society) or one built on the principles of social exclusion and isolation. Numerically and perhaps spiritually we have more segregation today than a decade ago. When 90 percent of the public school children of Washington are Negro, it is a farce to speak of integration, and Washington happens to be only the front runner among our cities. In Atlanta some 6000 Negro children now attend public schools with whites, but a majority of these are in schools with only the merest handful of white children. In 1954 over 27,000 Negro children attended all-Negro schools; in 1961, the first year of desegregation, about 48,000 attended all-Negro schools; today the number is higher than ever before. In the new ways of some Southern school boards, racial breakdowns are no longer released, but simple arithmetic shows that at least 53,000 Negro children are being educated now in completely segregated schools. Desegregation is lagging far behind population increase. While this has been happening, the total white enrollment in Atlanta's public schools moved from 54,000 in 1954 to only 59,000 in 1961: today the number can hardly be over 50,000. In 1954, Negroes were about 33 percent of total enrollment; today in Atlanta they are about 55 percent and the white enrollment has declined numerically as well as proportionately. All over the country the story is much the same, as the white population steadily migrates from the central city.

The Southern segregationists had known all along that the issue was not civil rights but integration. We must all realize this. Racism once lost a war but won the peace by substituting segregation for slavery. Racism is losing another war, but unless integration is the outcome it will again win the peace.

Of perhaps only one thing, other than change itself, can we be sure. Whatever the new patterns are, they will not simply evolve. The new patterns will, piece by piece, be consciously built up. In this field men are literally making their own history.

I stated earlier that the Negro had been his own keenest adversary. This was not meant unkindly. We should remember that even the name "Negro" is a white man's word, and that his whim conferred it on Africans transported here. Not only was the Negro given his name by white men, but in a measure his identity as well. He was taught, systematically and carefully, to doubt his own worth and made to fear the possibility that the white man's valuation of his worth might be correct. Every force of economics, politics, and psychology restrained him from full discovery of his own talents and inner strength. If to the white man he was, as Ralph Ellison said, invisible,[13] to

[13]George Orwell had also talked of this phenomenon in other settings; see his essays, "Marrakech" and "Looking Back on the Spanish War."

himself he was unrevealed. Now in this era of change we have not only or even chiefly a reform of laws and practices, but a mighty outpouring of dammed up human spirits, no longer massed and still and unknown even to themselves but rushing for their own levels. The surge of Negro Americans for self-fulfillment has shaken America loose from its complacency and forced self-examination on it. And while America as a whole learns from this the worst about itself, Negro Americans are, finally, learning the best about themselves.

In the foregoing two chapters, I have tried to convey some of the Promethean quality of our time in the United States. Some have read Karl Marx to assert that when the class struggle ends with the final and perfect victory of the proletariat, then history in a Marxist understanding will end, because, freed at last of class warfare, men will no longer be determined by history but will determine it. Such a concept, if indeed Marx held it, is too abstract to be intelligible to those who are themselves too involved in historical action to be concerned with concepts such as "determination," that have an existence only in the lamplight of brooding minds.

Yet there is suggestiveness here. Societies in many parts of the world have been beset by certain issues indigenous to them, and when these are at last subdued there is the potential for a general release of energy for new tasks. I say "potential" because this is speculation, since precedents do not occur to me of societies which have managed to keep themselves intact despite the internal pressure of great divisive issues until finally those issues were mastered.

Would it be foolishly optimistic to wonder whether this is not the situation imminent in the United States? Almost from its birth the republic had three grand issues to resolve; in later years a fourth has been added. A history of the frontier, the corporation, and the Negro, and of the country's response to each, would embrace nearly all of the American experience. We occupied the frontier. The corporation has been articulated into the social and political order, though problems of economic power and the relationship of corporate power to the political process still are with us and will be forever. And now it seems to me that in bringing Southern separatism nearly to an end and in moving at long last to accept the constitution and its command that Negroes are in right and in fact citizens, we have the opportunity to resolve the oldest of all the original issues, and that is the Negro.

The new thematic problem which came before we were ready for it concerns, of course, America's place and responsibility in the world. We shall be long resolving this issue, if we ever do. But I take confidence from the belief that the distance we have so far gained on the race question does release our minds and our institutions for a more clear-headed definition and management of foreign policies.

Beyond that, is it foolishly optimistic to think that an America which no longer need be seared by war within itself, nor by a sense of faithlessness to its own avowed principles, can now devote itself to making this a land that has a special care for each individual within it? As a matter of fact, no lesser goal would match the dreams of the civil-rights movement.

I do not know, nor can anyone, how long the qualities that today inhere in Negro Southerners may continue. I do know that these men and women now have a distinctiveness. This is a new body of people entering the midcurrent of American life, bringing with them an élan, a vigor, an infusion of uniquely phrased talents. In a sense these old Americans are our contemporary immigrants, imparting as did earlier waves of immigrants their own fresh vitality and ideas and style to the nation.

Remarkably, they are steeped in the pristine ideals of this democracy. They have invoked America pure against America defiled. They are wonderfully varied in opinions and aspirations, yet their characteristic thrust is toward the ideal. Historians and social scientists may explain this, but some mystery there will still be. Do we judge the South by its meanness or by its production of men and women such as those who have inspirited and led us these last years? What is the essential South? Is it the home that sends forth George Wallace or that sends forth Martin Luther King?

What in the life and history of the South bred the spirits that have seldom demanded their rights, as they have every justification for doing, as simple birthright? One almost never hears or reads that. One finds instead a demand for rights because Christianity, or American ideals, or even the economy or our foreign relations, requires that they be recognized. Is this again only the old Negro deference, not putting himself forward simply as a person? Perhaps. Perhaps, however, out of old humbling experiences Negroes learned something deep about the requirements of self-respect, learned that the self can sustain its integrity only if it is steadily loyal to great, integrating, communal values.

These are strange revolutionaries. They come as defenders of the land and its values. They come, as one prominent white Southerner once put it to me, to give us back our country. They revolt by defending the constitution against violation, defending national ideals against cheapening, defending Christianity against faithlessness, the economy against disruption, and foreign influence against vulnerability. Immigrants from home, revolutionaries in behalf of old loyalties.

There are Southern places—Albany, Americus, Birmingham, Selma, Bogalusa, and others—that have endured conflict fierce and unreconciled, and the social wounds from these will be long in healing. But the direction and momentum of Southern affairs is no longer in such places. Elsewhere, change is welcomed, often awkwardly, sometimes gracelessly, frequently skillfully accepted. In this South of fluidity the special qualities of America's new immigrants will leaven and give value to the South's first encounter with democracy.

III

★ ★ ★ ★ ★

The Liberal Temper

THE WORDS "liberalism" and "liberal" (both as adjective and noun) are in a pathetic state: one hardly knows whether to describe them as meaningless or meaningful. They are promiscuous words. So many suitors have seduced them and so many attackers have raped them that whatever meanings they have not already given birth to they seem to be pregnant with. We do not yet, however, have useful replacements for them. We have to make do with them, even though when we do we often muddy more than we clarify.

Liberals—whoever they are—are contemporarily in bad repute. The political left sneers at them, Negro polemicists bait them, segregationists snarl at them, and the political right accuses them of every imaginable sin. One of the favorite beliefs of the latter two groupings is that liberals now rule the country. On this, I agree with them. Liberals are now ascendant in this country and have the responsibilities that go with rule. This implies that they must concede that their ancient function of being critics of rulers is being modified, and they must tolerate the thought that the socially indispensable role of criticism now falls primarily to the conservative opponents of the liberal ruling class.

Inasmuch as almost no liberal is psychically capable of agreeing that he is a member of the ruling class, some description of liberalism is here required. As already noted, the word is in such chaos that many definitions, convenient to the proof of many hypotheses, are plausible. Liberals are like Chevrolets. There was a time when one could, with easily acquired experience, infallibly recognize a Chevrolet; models changed from year to year, but they still had a common resemblance. Today the variety of Chevrolets approaches infinity. Surface resemblances with older models and with other models of the same year are practically nonexistent, and only the faithful or the experts can believe or know that under the hood traditional and common values still live. The one clear and distinct quality that distinguishes a Chevrolet from another line is that it calls itself a Chevrolet, though typically now not very proudly and only as an afterthought; it seems to prefer to be differentiated from others by species and not genus. So it is with liberals. Are we back to Spencer's law, of progress from homogeneity to differentiation?

Turning somewhat fearfully from that prospect,[1] let me—on the side of homogeneity—venture a work-

[1]Accordingly I shall avoid in this and the subsequent chapters newly bright and ingenious coinages and try instead to get by with generic terms, such as "liberal," "radical," and "pragmatic," blunted and colorless as they may be.

able description of modern American liberalism, not a *definition* of it, for that would be far too hard.

A recognizably distinct group of citizens has held together for a good many years, despite disagreements over particular questions, around four general convictions. These men and women are satisfied with the economic policies and directions of the New Deal and accept them as a given in American life; at the same time, they are cautious about going beyond or outside these directions. They affirm America's world responsibilities and favor the growth of international cooperation. They shun ideological commitments in either economic or political theory. They believe in the First and Fourteenth Amendments. A fifth conviction, or lack of one, could almost be added: these same people tend not to be especially religious, though they can tolerate those of their number who are.

These men and women rule this country. They rule not only in the great, gray Washington palaces, but they more or less predominate in our banks, universities, media, foundations, trade unions, churches, and even industries. People who want to repeal the New Deal or to go far beyond it, who want drastically less international cooperation, who are ideological in their political and economic views, who are usually suspicious of the First and Fourteenth Amendments, and who are religiously centered are not widespread in the ruling class.

What I have described as the liberal reflects, of course, the political opinions generated by the New Deal. Its era is not yet closed, though it is likely that we are at its culmination. What I have described as the cardinal opinions of the liberal are all ideas and attitudes conditioned by and congenial to urban life. It seems quite likely that the civilization of cities now has more influence on political attitudes than class distinction has. The cities take hold of their people and rub them to fit. In basic beliefs and habitual outlook city dwellers of all classes tend to be more similar to each other than any of them are to rural and small-town people—unless a class like the ghettoized Negroes is kept semipermanently in degrading circumstances, as was the proletariat of nineteenth-century Europe.

I do not say that this liberal ruling class will hold sway forever, and I have already implied that we may be near the end of an era, beyond which new divisions may arise. But it is true that for the past thirty years liberalism has been in ascendancy. The Eisenhower administration had heretical tendencies, but that is all they really were. The heresy involved some pernicious doubts about the wisdom of the individual freedom which the First Amendment symbolizes, together with an incipient but usually frustrated inclination to court political and economic ideology: Messrs. Dulles, Benson, Summerfield, and other of the Eisenhower lieutenants were never allowed by the real world to be as doctrinaire in act as they would have liked.

Some of President Johnson's critics from within the liberal camp have made the word "consensus" a term of derision. The President has been more discerning than they. He has understood what the politics of the post-1932 years has been about, and what a broad field of agreement has been formed within the public. He has understood also the bounds of it.

There is, of course, strongly voiced dissent within liberal ranks. It has been less about basic issues, on which disagreement is narrow, than about particular policies and about power. The liberal consensus embraces so many people and so much power that it breeds its own subgroups and subprograms. These produce real contests that are often of crucial importance. They are the stuff of contemporary politics, but the disagreements and contests, though frequently intense, have been imprecise as to principle and blurred as to division.

This is, as yet, true as well for the disagreements over foreign policies. Among these the only practically serious threat to the continuance of the consensus appears to be the question of our response to external communism. Other foreseeable disagreements about foreign policies could almost surely be resolved within the consensus. Until quite recently, so could disagreements regarding external communism. There had developed a general acceptance of the principles that American power should be employed to restrict the further spread of communist control of states but that, at the same time, there could be gradual accommodations with those states where communist control was already well established. The Vietnam war pushed us back to a rethinking of this position. The debate could fragment the liberal consensus, because the war has provided a cause and an outlet for moral judgment, a charge that radical irresponsibility infects governmental decision-making on war and peace. Some of the fine nonviolent credo of the civil-rights movement moved into the Vietnam epic, merging there with a devoted identification with the hurt of all impoverished people, a sensitivity nurtured also within the Negro revolt; the controversy was thereby made to transcend the specific case and to become a quest for democratic purposes in foreign affairs. The Vietnam protest has produced some awful exhibitions of bad tempers, bad manners, and vicious scape-goating, but the finer qualities that inhere in it have made it a remarkable thing.

It became all the more remarkable because of the reception it found. In the civil-rights controversy, important elements of social leadership were responsive to the moral challenge raised by the civil-rights militants. Just as impressively, members of the leadership joined the Vietnam opposition. Civil rights, as a cause, never belonged exclusively to radical opinion; nor did Vietnam. In both cases ruling-class liberals adopted and to a considerable degree gave their form and stamp to a cause originating out of radical protest. They did so in part because of shared ideals and in part because their always latent pragmatic intelligence was affronted by the irrationality of segregation and of romantic foreign policies. There could hardly be a stronger witness of the contemporary resilience and vitality of the liberal spirit.

The liberal camp is not united on the great question thrust forward and crystalized by Vietnam, and the division could widen into an irreparable one, which could severely weaken if not destroy the capability of carrying forward economic and other reforms. As of this time (March 1966), I doubt the likelihood of this outcome—short of a decisive military reversal or a similar national humiliation. The more probable development would seem to be tightly organized and active criticism, within the consensus, on this one issue, representing both the views of greater firmness and of greater flexibility toward external communism.

Yet this is to conjecture merely the probable, and if we have learned from experience with the civil-rights controversy we should by now have an awareness that we can move farther than we may prudently think we can. Vietnam has unwound our minds. It can bring us more speedily to resolution of the grand thematic problem of America's responsibility to other peoples of the world. From its torturing impact signs already emerge of a willingness to confront and re-examine the ideological sanctities of our foreign policies; if we do succeed in subduing these ideological fogs we might be enabled to get rid also of the sentimentality that pervades other expressions of our foreign policies—for example, in Africa—and even the robber-baron spirit that has so long dominated our relations with Latin America.

What makes the present moment auspicious is, I suggest, the confluence of three factors. First, the long-established agenda of modern liberalism is now fairly completed. The New Deal is well assimilated, our commitment to international cooperation is firm, pramatism is ingrained, and constitutional rights are being defended. Second, the discovery by the moral judgment that always exists within liberalism of a concrete issue—Vietnam—on which to fructify produces the seeds for a creative definition of new political alignments. Third, the enfranchisement of Negroes and the spread of reapportionment—both items on the liberal agenda—*promise* overwhelming freedom of action for years to come for the liberal camp.

This promise depends heavily on whether the controversy over external communism can be contained. It depends also on whether the new items being added to the liberal agenda by the Negroes can be expeditiously achieved. If they are not, Negro voters may congregate within one of the parties—and, of course, most likely within the Democratic Party—as a discordant bloc. It seems not at all difficult to conceive of an Adam Clayton Powell and a group like him playing an obstructionist role within the Democratic Party functionally similar to that of Southerners like Byrd and Eastland in the past.

I hope it is clear that I am not identifying liberalism with the Democratic Party. Events may do that, but need not. A Republican Party built on the same liberal tenets can, as it has in the past, effectively compete for office and power. Built on any other basis, it will stay out of national power unless some great domestic or international catastrophe ruptures the liberal consensus. The right wing may very possibly grow larger and stronger, but its future is criticism and opposition, not rule, unless a disaster comparable to the Depression of the 1930's, which brought liberals to ascendancy, occurs.

Conservatives are today's primary critics and dissenters. They are the true rebels. The young radical protesting America's intervention in Vietnam undoubtedly thinks of himself as a rebel, and in a way he is, but in not much of a way, for the evidence seems clear that the Vietnam opposition is centered predominantly within a general commitment to liberal politics. Excepting for some few seeking to create a new political perspective, the ambition of the dissident is merely to influence the ruling class's policies. The true rebels want to displace the ruling class and take over its power; and these rebels are on the right.

As critics and dissenters are socially valuable, we have an interest in how well conservatives take up the role that liberals have so long fulfilled. It is a great pity, therefore, that the conservative critics are generally inept; there is none among them who matches the best of liberal self-criticism—say that of Mr. Paul Goodman. Among the conservatives, Mr. William Buckley is always intelligent and frequently interesting, but too playful to be provocative. Mr. Russell Kirk is erudite, but a man who is against almost every change is hardly credible. Mr. William S. White's advocacy is suffocatingly sentimental, and his attacks are insufferably malicious. Mr. David Lawrence, unlike most conservative commentators, has genuine respect for facts and is readable, but from day to day one finds it hard to remember what he said. One can remember what Mr. Arthur Krock says, but somehow one also remembers the point he missed in the law case he is expounding. Mr. C. P. Ives of the Baltimore *Sun* is invariably stimulating, but, like a true philosophical conservative, he is content to stay in his locality and is little read elsewhere. Mr. Kilpatrick, the Richmond champion of massive resistance, exemplifies at its most purple the current fashion in conservative literature of writing so lushly adorned with pseudo-Burkisms as to be almost gagging in its pretentiousness.

Conspicuous in the South's recent rebellion has been the almost total absence, the artful Mr. Kilpatrick aside, of any reasoned, intelligent defense of its position. There was virtually no intellectual debate. I have for a number of years read the writings of the segregationists, and I can remember only two writers—neither of them a professional—who presented arguments that caused me to rethink any position. This may merely evidence my dogmatism, but I suspect that few other readers found even two. One of the writers was the New Orleans Catholic, Emile Wagner, in his little publicized letters to the Catholic hierarchy.[2] The other was Senator Fulbright, in his *amicus* views before the Supreme Court in the 1958 case of *Cooper* v. *Aaron;*[3] the Senator was brief if impressive, and never, as far as I know, returned to the subject again.

Against critics such as these, the quality of modern liberalism towers high. In twentieth-century America's hunger for self-analysis we have gorged ourselves on damning self-criticism and anxious discovery and invention of neuroses. The tapeworms are still in our intestines and probably ought to be. But accurate self-examination requires an assessment of strengths as well as weaknesses, and we may as well entertain the

[2]They are discussed in James G. Cook, *The Segregationists* (New York: Appleton-Century-Crofts, 1962), pp. 229–46.
[3]358 U.S. 1. See *Congressional Record* for August 23, 1958, p. 19852.

thought, which I believe historians of the future will confirm, that modern men, in their American variety, have done some things well.

We have been caught in the terrifying dilemmas of the cold war and have lived in the presence of the bomb, and yet have kept our sanity. We have shown a capacity, which nothing in American history would have forecast, to set ourselves enormous national tasks —such as to guard half the world—and to see them through with patient resolve and without overreaction to criticism. We have lived in a condition of constant military alert and yet, in defiance of the precedents furnished by other peoples in such circumstance, have steadily expanded the legal protections of free speech and dissent. We have fairly successfully kept under control the original sin of all political behavior—the desire to substitute ideology for free thought and political myths for pragmatic goals. We have confronted the question of equality and have thus challenged humanity's original sin, which is, as theologians of all faiths and philosophers of many persuasions tell us, pride and presumption. We have supplied a strong measure of determination to see through the process of making equality actual, and we are doing this in the racial category, where almost no other community of people has ever achieved impressive results or even shown much desire to. We have announced a resolve to do something equally unprecedented in mankind's annals—to abolish poverty. These things are not the marks of a decadent society.

So let us not flinch from facing our virtues. Forty-odd years ago, Albert Schweitzer wrote: "We are called upon for a single kind of effort only, and have to work like men who are rebuilding the damaged foundations of a cathedral under the weight of the massive building."[4] The cathedral has had to bear unimaginable punishment in the intervening years, and yet it still stands. Unless it be an illusion, we have still a civilized order. Possibly, we have lost some humanity along the way, a way that took us through two world wars and much else besides. We have looked into the yawning pit of barbarism, have learned with dismay how simple it is for men to step backward into it and to forsake in a moment the pinnacle of civilization which required centuries to raise. And so no class of persons is more critically important to a culture than its historians, for they teach that this dilemma is not uniquely modern, but is of all time and is within men's power to surmount. As the historians work to keep uneroded the isthmus between what men have done and what men are now confronted with, they make the contribution, which only they can, to the prevention or eradication of the sense of loneliness and despair lurking in wait for any generation unable to convert the oppression of the past into assimilated history. The instruction of history is that every age and not just our own has been in a perilous condition, that men have always had to labor to create purposeful existences, and that this effort has been as it is now the only defense against barbarism.

It is absolutely necessary to know this in order to possess self-respect and to be protected against the

[4] *The Decay and Restoration of Civilization*, trans. by C. T. Campion (New York: Macmillan, 1923), p. 72.

anxiety which springs so readily when the world seems implacably menacing and unfriendly. The ancient Greeks argued the problem of nature vs. convention, and in one style or another the same question has always been with thinking men. It is the problem of whether our values—moral, political, aesthetic—are naturally right, or whether they are the mere products of convention. Of course they stem from convention. This recognition does not, however, necessarily negate their truthfulness.

What men have built through their thought and action—now monumentalized as institutions, beliefs, and values—does not merit disparagement. The human mind lusts for certainties: this is one of the indecencies of our nature. Men are obsessed with pride in everything that they do except what they do with their most ardent and serious intent: the fashioning of the values they live by. As regards this, they are humble and ashamed and typically want to credit these values to God or to some myth. The humility is proper, but not the shame, and it will not be covered by the cloak of absolutes. To foist the origin of our values on the absolute is disrepect both for God and ourselves.

What history teaches is that values are conventions, resulting from the thirst for purpose of the generations of mankind, filtered through the critical intelligence of men and taking their adequacy and truth from the improvement of that filter, occasionally becoming gross and impure because the filter has been allowed to clog or its fiber to break. This realization means self-respect. It means reconciliation with the world through union with the age-old endeavor to fashion a purposeful world by imparting value and meaning to it. It means that we know ourselves to be the sole arbiters between civilization and barbarism.

This has been the constant faith of liberalism. Up to this point, I have talked of liberalism as a political force. It is time to define it as an idea, and an old formulation by G. H. Sabine seems as helpful toward a definition as any. "Throughout its history liberalism has been first and foremost a belief in the supreme social value of intelligence."[5] This is a conclusion which conservatism cannot accept. It is the taproot of the philosophical distinction between the two. However alike they may sometimes be in particulars, the conservative rebels at thrusting his beliefs into the strait jacket of logic. The liberal freely accepts it as his security. It is perhaps naive to trust that intelligence is a match for the barbaric forces which inhere in men and societies. But the liberal has always been naive, and his naiveté is and has been the bootstraps of the species. His has been the humanistic faith that, though the salvation of men may be through the grace of God, men's welfare and happiness are not, for they come if at all only through self-reliance.

It follows that the liberal is set far apart from all political mythmakers, whether of the left or the right, for the liberal believes in an open society of exploring individuals, and they in prescriptive political truth. It follows that liberalism is at eternal enmity with what Socrates had long ago sorrowfully named "misology" —the hatred of ideas. Nor can it ever acquiesce in the

[5] "The Historical Position of Liberalism," *The American Scholar*, Winter 1940–41, p. 49.

command of Amaziah to Amos: "Go, flee away to the land of Judah, and eat bread there, and prophesy there; but never again prophesy at Bethel, for it is the king's sanctuary." With Amos the liberal believes there are no sanctuaries privileged from inquiry.[6] He has learned to be suspicious of the tolerance of political powers for intelligence. He is also more than a little skeptical of the reliability of those who are reputed experts; he is attentive to them and grateful when they instruct, but he suspects that the murkiness of their language is frequently not accidental. But equally, he distrusts with Kant the "innocence" of common sense, which is at all times "easily seduced."[7] The liberal has, therefore, taken seriously the warnings of those who have spoken of the tyranny of the crowd; he has, nonetheless, opted for democracy, because he abhors unmerited privilege. He knows that democracy has less respect for him than he for it, that when it embarks to make the world safe for democracy, to control subversives, even to abolish poverty and end discrimination, or to accomplish any of its similar urgent missions, it inevitably tends to adopt the old precept that justice is the interest of the stronger; nor is he surprised when the endeavor somehow bypasses its objective and overruns him. He will, finally, agree with Santayana that "the virtue of liberalism is a sort of intellectual kindness or courtesy to all possible wills."[8]

[6] Amos 7:12–17.
[7] "Metaphysical Foundations of Morals," in C. J. Friedrich, ed., *The Philosophy of Kant* (New York: Modern Library, 1949), p. 153.
[8] *Dominations and Powers* (New York: Scribners, 1951), p. 436.

Of all his qualities, none is more characteristic than the escape from ideology. Modern liberalism has become determinedly pragmatic. Even its commitment to equality and free speech seem to derive from an appraisal of social utility, though only in part, because modern liberalism combines a thick strand of idealism with its pragmatism. The special kind of devotion which Adlai Stevenson and John F. Kennedy attracted came from the way each in his own way personified the style of contemporary liberals: highly intelligent, habitually analytical, given to hard work, cool under pressure, disposed only toward clearly feasible solutions, skeptical of proposals whose full range of consequences they could not see, curious about but detached from ideas, unselfconsciously idealistic but self-protective against illusion.

I have already made clear that the avoidance of ideology seems to rank among the very highest of political values. An ideological politics means a politics that can deal with human problems only according to creedal truth, a politics intolerant of dissent and subordinating human wants and needs to the sanctity of assured principles. We endured a relatively mild form of ideological politics throughout America during the 1920's, and a vicious form in the South until the present.

A liberalism that has emancipated itself from ideology needs still, however, some unifying explanations of the political order, and radical critics, of both left and right, are uncomfortably close to the truth in their accusation that our politics is empty of value. We are dangerously short of theory. Modern liberalism

still recites as its ideals old refrains from the political
litany of the seventeenth and eighteenth centuries,
but the philosophical underpinning of those themes
has been long since rejected by both intellectuals and
laity. The self-evident truths of the Declaration of
Independence are intelligible only in the light of seven-
teenth-century concepts, concepts now widely disbe-
lieved, of man as a rational nature and truth as clear
and distinct. We have not replaced these concepts
with others that integrate the liberal values we pro-
fess and serve, and the anxiety and pain from this lack
of comprehension are plainly evident. Some people
have sought such concepts in religion, where I think
they cannot be found, and in sentiment and sentimentality, where I know they cannot be found. The
closest we have come to a philosophical perspective
widely shared and permeating our practice was probably the pragmatism of John Dewey. But the great
shortcoming of Dewey, his predecessors, and his fol-
lowers was that they too frequently tended to regard
difficult questions as unanswerable, and hence to
ignore them. Besides being fundamentally illiberal,
this tendency was pragmatically weak; people living in
a world as disturbed as is ours preeminently want help
with hard questions, for they are not in short supply.

A great philosopher, in tune with his age and its
concerns, once redirected our civilization's thought by
erasing from his mind all that he had learned, and
starting over again from the single affirmation: "I
think, therefore I exist." The youth of the civil-rights
movement attempted something similar. They—Negro and white—doubted all and started anew by saying

in effect: "I know that I am not free, and therefore I know that freedom is possible." Perhaps they were the bearers of a new Cartesian revolution. Perhaps out of their search for a free life and from their conviction that the search must confirm in concepts only what it first discovers in action, we may begin to see again why there are some truths which are self-evident.

But this is the age-old cry of those who protest: "I am not free, therefore freedom is possible." There has been something, however, about this surge of thought which has tempted one to wonder if it might not be historic. The youth of the civil-rights movement did, after all, lead us to accept our constitution. Perhaps they can do more than that. They may lead us not only to make progress in integrating the races of men, but to find the thought that integrates life. Such great integrating thought has in the past come at times of historic crises, and this is, after all, the generation that came at the time of Hiroshima and has lived its entire life within the New World created by that moral as well as nuclear explosion. This Hiroshima generation seems to me to have a rather overblown streak of narcissism, but if it does not fall victim to that its career should be exciting. What seems to be its central idea—that valid thought derives only from action—is not, of course, of its own invention, but these younger men and women nourished in the civil-rights movement appear to be exploring it devotedly.

A determination to find truth only in the choices and commitments of direct personal involvement is a course with easy exits in puerile exhibitionism or maleficent romanticism. It can assail the most majestic of all human achievements, which is the acceptance of the discipline of logic. It could in the South—which knew without having ever heard of existentialism that knowing the truth came only from testing it against life—lead merely to a withholding of judgment. But seen as a means to the discovery (*not* the creation) of credible truths, it is a philosophical affirmation that offers release from the sterility of thought which is withdrawn from the human endeavor to build cultures satisfyingly integrated by understood values.

The pragmatic bias, manifold as are its benefits, contains the inner susceptibility for decay of present liberalism. This modern Puritanism glorifies work, without old Puritanism's comprehension that men's lives and work are subject to higher authority. Liberalism has lost its sense of authoritative purpose, and too many of its adherents are in consequence lonely, abstracted men.

The pragmatic bias exposes the liberal ruling class to other dangers of a more tangibly political sort, which are discussed at some length in Chapter IV. They grow from liberalism's good motives and are therefore especially difficult to be wary of or to combat. One is the tendency to separate leadership from constituents and the other is the liberal obsession (and that is not too strong a word) with rights.

The pragmatic liberal tends to make existing institutions work instead of changing them, tends to be interested only in clearly feasible solutions. Nevertheless, he retains his distinction from the conservative: he believes, in contrast to the conservative, that all problems should be solved or at least treated. When the conservative does seek to do something about a problem that can no longer be tolerated, he looks for solutions that respect existing interests; in contrast, the pragmatic liberal typically looks for solutions that bypass existing interests and create new ones.

Thus, to give but one example, the pragmatic liberal denominational leaders of the Protestant churches, faced during the Negro revolt with the racism of their congregations, have made but half-hearted efforts to minister to those congregations, to remind them that the Gospel means, if it means anything at all, that the true church is those who believe themselves to be new men and thus reconciled with all creation. Instead of seeking to reform their congregations directly, the Protestant leaders have given their greater energies to going outside them, witnessing in the streets of Selma or Chicago or the cloakrooms of Congress, perhaps hoping thereby to form new congregations around themselves that will counterbalance the established ones, but above all contending for the freedom of leadership to act independently of the will of the constituent body.

We admire this as courage and as responsible use of position, yet when it becomes prevalent in one social field after another, its result is deep alienation between the power holders of a society and the masses.

Similarly, liberalism's oldest concern is to protect the individual against governing powers, even if they are supported by popular majorities. In America this has led to a concentration on constitutional rights. Every good motive is capable of excess, and the temptation here is that liberals forget that a right is a defense against social power, not a prescription of the kind of society there must be. When we twist the concept of rights to require that institutions be of a certain kind, we take a step that is fundamentally illiberal, because rather than acknowledging rights we are creating vested interests. To give only one example, in the Colorado reapportionment case, the Supreme Court, to the applause of liberals, held that:

> Except as an interim remedial procedure justifying a court in staying its hand temporarily, we find no significance in the fact that a nonjudicial, political remedy may be available for the effectuation of asserted rights to equal representation in a state legislature. . . . We hold that the fact that a challenged legislative apportionment plan *was approved by the electorate* is without federal constitutional significance, if the scheme adopted fails to satisfy the basic requirements of the Equal Protection Clause, as delineated in our opinion in *Reynolds* v. *Sims.*[9]

Can this be the authentic voice of liberalism? How—consistent with the liberal tradition—can we say that an individual has legal right to a particular kind of governmental structure? Liberalism has time and again denied that justice is the interest of the stronger. In its day of rule, this ought still to be its precept.

[9] *Lucas* v. *Colorado General Assembly,* 377 U.S. 713, 736–37. Italics supplied.

The liberal banner belongs to the present liberal camp only by sufferance. It cannot be expected it will always stay there. Today, the consensus yielded out of the momentum of the New Deal is vast, secure, affluent, and habituated to power. It embodies, for the present, convictions and policies not uncongenial to the liberal spirit, but it is too grand and powerful for anyone to believe positively that it can long remain devoted to the "supreme social value of intelligence" and practice an "intellectual kindness or courtesy to all possible wills."

Whenever the liberal majority wavers far from these qualities, the liberal spirit will move elsewhere, to represent on other fronts the requirements of freedom. "Liberty," Croce once wrote in a beautiful passage, "demands ideas and ideals, and the infinite sky, and the background of the universe, not as extraneous to man but as the very spirit that thinks and works within him and joyfully creates ever new forms of life."[10] The ascendancy of American liberalism, climaxed by the civil-rights victories, has created new and better forms of life. We have a valid chance to make of this republic a society in which each man can attain his self-fulfillment. If for a while longer—a decade or so at least—the present ruling class can be kept responsive to the liberal spirit, we may make this chance fuller and fairer.

[10] Benedetto Croce, *History of Europe in the Nineteenth Century*, trans. by Henry Furst (New York: Humanities Press, 1933), p. 258.

IV

★ ★ ★ ★ ★

Federal Policies

AFTER THE 1954 decision, the eleven Southern states, with varying measures of vigor, challenged national authority; parts of six other states—Delaware, Kentucky, Maryland, Missouri, Oklahoma, and West Virginia—also did, occasionally. The challenge was four times actually carried by states to the point of a display of armed forces: at Mansfield, Texas, in 1956, at Little Rock in 1957, at the University of Mississippi in 1962, and at the University of Alabama in 1963. An ordeal such as this could not but put the federal system under severe strain.

Given the nature of the contest, it had to be an especially stressful experience, and we may not for some time know what the aftereffects will be. We have no X rays for the body politic. We can probe only with our minds, scanning the surfaces of things, relating the signs we see with what we presume to know about constitutions.

Our political literature is full of discussions of the place of an organized minority within a democratic political order. A few conclusions come from these discussions and from practical experience with which there may be general agreement.

First, all might agree that a democracy presupposes that the majority can require a minority to accept its procedurally correct decisions as to the public interest. Many would accept this statement without qualification. Many others, while accepting, would desire an explicit recognition that "procedurally correct" means among other things full observance of individual constitutional rights.

Second, experience suggests at least two considerations which ought to moderate the imposition of this ultimate majoritarian power; one of these is the extreme difficulty that large and complex societies have in ascertaining and verifying the majority opinion on any question; another is the practical as well as moral desirability of a minimal use of coercive power over fellow citizens.

Third, most persons would have to acknowledge, even if they wished otherwise, that minority coercion is especially inexpedient when the minority is approximately identical with a territorial area, and the disadvantages are even greater when, in a federal system, the minority is approximately identical with one or more of the federal units.

Finally, when the minority is defending a notion of right or morality, rather than merely a notion of interest, all of the cautions against majority coercion speak more loudly.

What has made the civil-rights controversy such a serious test of the inner strength of American federal institutions is that all of the warning flags were down. No one knew or could know that an actual majority of Americans, or even voters, opposed legal segregation; some measure of coercion was demonstrably required; the minority was itself the predominant power within a large and compact segment of the country; its power was enhanced and legitimatized by the constitutional status of federal units; and a very large part of the controversy was and is between competing notions of right and morality.

Entangled by all these complicating and debilitating factors, the federal system has nevertheless held intact, the flag still flies, the law's writ still runs. Can we not say, therefore, that this republic met its trial and met it sufficiently well?

Or should we, on the contrary, hold that the record of these last ten or so years convicts federalism, at least its American variety, of intolerable inadequacy? A plausible case could be argued that federalism allowed and even created the conflict, that without federalism we could have long ago subdued the race problem. An even more plausible case can be made on the grounds that the past decade demonstrated the frightful capacity for obstruction and turmoil inherent in a federal structure.

These arguments probably could not be cogently defeated by direct rebuttal. One can but demur to them and state a counterbalancing case for American federalism. The force of the arguments can be qualified, however, if not rebutted, by recalling that the nation as a whole did not feel a compelling urgency to end the controversy until Negro Southerners, beginning in 1960, took to the streets. Indeed, not before the Birmingham events of 1963 did civil rights become a primary interest of Washington. A high-ranking administration official wrote to me in a letter dated February 1963: "It is not possible to get school desegregation legislation through Congress this year. Next year may be a different question: I do not know. . . . I have to accept as a starting point that under [present] circumstances Congress simply will not pass a school desegregation bill. . . . On the other hand, I am afraid that problems of law enforcement in some places, before the free exercise of the franchise, are almost insurmountable at present under the federal system."

In June 1963, at a White House conference with leaders of the civil-rights movement, one of them spoke strongly about Birmingham Police Commissioner Connor. President Kennedy interrupted, and with his fine and disarming irony said, "Don't be too hard on Bull Connor. If it weren't for him, we wouldn't be here today."

This is, after all, nothing new, even if saddening. A great work of historical research still waits to be done on the role of shock in human affairs, and Birmingham was the shock this nation took flight from. In a desperate striving for understanding and remedial action, the Negro movement time and time again has sought to produce shock. Sometimes it has succeeded, as at Birmingham and Selma, but the lesson of those places all too plainly shows that the American conscience is more affrighted by the villainy of a Connor or a Sheriff Clark than it is summoned by the appeal of heroic men and women.

What do we make of this tactic that the civil

rights movement discovered, this use of the streets? Is it a new and useful method of rendering a modern government responsible? A few months ago a Negro of fifty-odd years said to me, "These young people have done more good in a couple of years than we did all our lives." The remark was poignant and memorable because this was a man, one of many in the South, who had devoted a lifetime to working for change. He and his generation had had little to show for their efforts. And then younger Negroes took to the streets, and local governments and finally the government in Washington responded; industrial and financial chieftains responded; universities, which had been typically unconcerned and had felt no responsibility, responded: the start, for example, of the cooperative agreement idea, of which The University of Michigan–Tuskegee plan is one of more than a dozen examples, came in the wake of Birmingham. Even when street action has been riotous and destructive, it has created conditions which have induced authorities and community leaders to act in ways they had avoided before; the *Wall Street Journal* for October 5, 1965, reported at length on the newly found interest of Los Angeles civic and political leadership in the conditions of life in Watts. The *Journal* reporter quoted one Watts resident as saying: "The people here feel they had tried legal, peaceful means to state their cause. But with one phrase—'Burn, baby, burn' —they feel that got the attention that never came from years of pleading."[1]

---

[1] Attention, however, has not always been productive of improvements.

When Atlanta students marched for the first time, early in 1960, I went down to the sidewalk to watch. The elevator operator in our building was an elderly Negro woman, old-fashioned and traditional and fitting exactly the Southern stereotype of what a Negro matriarch—and she was that—should be. She stood beside me in the doorway as the students went by, whispering over and over again, "March on chillun, march on." Those early marches, those early sit-ins, seemed so right, so absolutely right and beautiful. To one who thought he knew the South and its people they were incredible, but they were also somehow sublimely natural.

From demonstrations of sober, impeccably dressed, always orderly Southerners of 1960 we have come a long and not necessarily better way, to the unkempt uniforms and antibourgeois themes of more recent protesters. Yet the essential truth is the same. The public demonstration of grievances and demands, whether or not they involve civil disobedience, seems a valid method of political action within the almost hopelessly complex processes of a modern political order. The eternal problem of every democracy is to ascertain its own will and to reach consensus. Demonstrations are a tactic, and as such either have or do not have pragmatic value. Insofar as direct action facilitates consensus, it is useful not only to the demonstrator but to the society itself. Insofar as direct action creates or strengthens passions that make consensus more difficult, it is of no use either to the demonstrator or to society.

Responsive as the powers of society have often been to street action, it is not a stable method of effecting change or influencing policy. With every victory it wins, its validity decreases, because each victory admits the oppressed a little farther within the sanctum where the normal and regular levers of social influence are. Power seeks its own level, and its level is the governance of coercive and directive institutions. With every efficacious direct protest against the institution, the protesting class comes closer to sharing in the control of the institution itself. It comes closer to being, indeed, a part of its favorite paper tigers, the "power structure" or "the establishment." Frequently, probably usually, those who advance into the circles of power are not the same persons who protested. The direct beneficiaries of the civil-rights movement are the new breed of emergent Negro politicians (especially in the South), the bureaucrats of the poverty programs and the governmental civil-rights agencies, and a few movement leaders who have cascaded into prominence. They personify, in total, the gradual obsolescence of protest and its replacement by institutional force—the absorption by society of what has fertilized its barren and eroded areas.

Parenthetically, we might note who has suffered from the civil-rights turmoil of the South. Typically, and with some very notable exceptions, two sorts of people have been most often and seriously victimized: poor Negroes and moderately well-to-do whites. The former have been maimed and killed, had their homes burned, their churches bombed, their jobs and credit terminated. More often than not, these disasters have happened to Negroes who themselves were not personally active in civil-rights causes. The other personal sufferers, the white moderates, have usually not been either. They have been men and women going about their affairs, when unexpectedly they were caught up by some issue on which, almost without intent, they have drawn a line, and as a result have been forced out of town and from their positions or their pulpits. Very few of the civil-rights movement leaders of upper echelons have suffered; even fewer of the segregationist leaders have. In fact, the positions of many of the former and at least as many of the latter have seemingly been enhanced.

Perhaps the preceding paragraph has not been a parenthesis, for considerations such as these freshen our perception of the intricacy of life. We are all diminished and made vulnerable by the weaknesses of our social order, just as we are all magnified by its strengths. When a society is seized by change as convulsive as the Negro revolt, who leads, who profits, who survives, who suffers is a matter of accident. We are all engaged. There comes a point in our understanding of revolutions when we recognize that we are all, every one of us, revolutionaries. The men who made airlines and telephones and television possible made Selma possible, for without their technology Selma could not have been. The Booker T. Washingtons reared and nourished the militants of the Student Non-Violent Coordinating Committee. The man who moves his family to the suburbs, away from the Negro and the poor, lights the matches of Watts. The sharecropper who bows and scrapes invites the night riders of the Klan. The parish priest who ignores the strife and promotes his church bazaar whets the envy of the outsider. We are all involved, and the revolution comes to each of us where he is. As Plato put it: "Whether a man falls into a small swimming-bath or into the middle of the mighty ocean, he has to swim all the same."[2]

The institutions and legal norms that are bad are not those that bound and define our particular ocean, or that make its waves rough, but those that keep us on the shore, or tether us from swimming as far as we might, or that strike at us from below. Some of the forms of American federalism have had these pernicious effects. It is necessary to correct these. But we should do so with the realism that knows that a perfectible institution is always to be preferred to a new one. What we must guard against is the man who thinks of politics and its institutions and its laws as something more than a means, against the conservative spirit that tends to reify and make a venerated totem of every norm, as well as against the rootless spirit that tends to want a new model each year.

To quarrel with the past is as foolish as to idealize it. To blame American federalism for the evil of racial oppression is as irrelevant as is the excusing of the oppression because of the sanctity of the federal system. There is too much of such excusing, I think, in Burke Marshall's *Federalism and Civil Rights.* The need is and has been to end the oppression and tethering of people: neither the historic forms of federalism nor, for that matter, the historic forms of jury trials should be allowed to make oppression permanent or even long lasting.

[2] *Republic* 453.

Mr. Marshall does suggest that the slowness of the federal machinery may in some cases have the beneficial effect of providing the requisite time for adequate reforms rather than merely superficial patches.[3] Perhaps in a long view this may be true. The drawn-out agony of civil rights and Negro disadvantage has wrenched at minds perhaps deeply enough so that, if we have corrected slowly, we may correct deeply and at the causes.

In the first years of the crisis, before 1957 and even after, the federal judiciary was almost alone as a governmental agent of reform. This was an impossibly exposed position for the courts, nor were court proceedings and judicial decrees well adapted for the task of effecting social reforms. In the outcome the federal courts have been joined by Congress, the federal executive, and numerous agents of state and local government. Has there ever before been such a determined mobilization of governmental power concentrated on a single domestic problem? One would surmise from it that there is an overwhelming national approval of the cause of integration.

And yet time after time, voters have said the opposite. So far, the most revealing referenda have been on the housing question, each one of which—in Berkeley, Tacoma, Seattle, Detroit, Akron, and statewide in California—has shown voters favoring retention of the privilege of discriminatory sale of homes.

It is almost impossible to know where the people stand on integration. Public opinion polls indicate at

[3] *Federalism and Civil Rights* (New York: Columbia University Press, 1964), p. 74.

best only what they may be thinking, not what they will decide among available real choices. Elections, except in the South, do not turn on the single issue of race, and in most of the South they no longer do. Referenda, on the other hand, are so far isolated from other questions that they give voters the luxury of irresponsible escape from all intersecting interests, and their results are frequently mischievous and self-defeating.

Yet granted this uncertainty, there are omnipresent signs that government may be ahead of populace. The political evidence indicates that there is in this country a firm popular consensus against all forms of legalized or legally protected segregation, against voting discrimination, and in favor of impartial and vigorous law enforcement. My own observation, and one can depend here on little more than his own reading of events, is that there is not such a consensus in behalf of some of the other positions the national and state governments have taken. Specifically, I doubt that majority opinion is sympathetic to restricting the freedom to discriminate of employers and owners of residences.

This is, I think, an interesting phenomenon, and it occurs in other institutions than government. Do the majority of Protestant and Catholic churchgoers endorse the positions taken by their denominational leaders and bureaus on civil rights and integration? One sees little evidence that they do. Is the majority of labor union members at one with national spokesmen regarding equal opportunity? Few if any labor leaders believe so, though in public they may say otherwise. If I am correct in these observations, they furnish puzzles for theorists of democracy. We were long ago taught that in modern corporations ownership had been separated from control. The situation of governments, churches, and unions is not the same, but there are resemblances as well as differences. The leaders of unions and church bodies somehow have come to accept and act on an accountability to constituencies other than their memberships; in doing so, they have lost large portions of the capability of committing their memberships to policy positions. The governmental situation is more complex, but we may note that despite the proliferation of state fair-employment and fair-housing laws, and the entrance into these areas by the federal government, there is virtual unanimity among students that these laws and regulations have so far been ineffectually enforced and that their timid enforcement is traceable to the lack of effective popular support.

The separation of leadership from its primary constituency is of great moment and likely to be even greater. We see another aspect of it in the campus reform movement since the Berkeley riots, for a primary complaint of the student protest is that university administrations—the institutional leaderships—have separated themselves from accountability to what is said to be their legitimate constituency, the student body. The tightening tension between vested institutional leadership and its ranks, of which churches, labor unions, and universities provide present-day examples, is the common ground between today's radical right and new radical left, uniting them in a resentful disaffection against opaque bureaucracies.

This is a vital sector within which the governmental organs of American federalism must function. They have themselves been in strain. Those which were malfunctioning have probably been strengthened, for they have been emancipated from old shackles. I refer, of course, to Congress and to the state governments of the South, both of which should now enjoy a flow of new energy and new talent. The federal courts and the federal executive, which have been at the center of the offensive, have been differently affected. They took to themselves responsibilities and enlargements of functions which were needful for the crisis, but which may prove hard to lay down and harmful if not cast off. In particular, I think there are valid causes for worry lest our federal judiciary be encouraged in partisanship and be led to overload itself. We should give thought, furthermore, to the possible consequences of bureaucratizing civil rights within the federal and state administrative departments.

Partisanship is not the same concern as that posed by the debate between judicial activists and those who counsel judicial restraint. It is a different question —that of the impartiality of the courts as between the parties at the bar. Judicial partiality in a trial court produces bad decisions; judicial partiality in appellate courts produces bad law. The federal courts became the forum of the bitterest and most emotional controversy of our time. On their performance not only the rights of parties but struggles for power have depended. We must all acknowledge the extraordinary record of some of the Southern federal judges as they have, under the worst possible conditions, defended the rule of law and the dignity of American government. At the same time, other federal judges in the South have made clear their own preeminent commitment to segregation and to the established political structures of Southern states and localities. To take one example of several which unfortunately could be cited, the handling of the Dallas school desegregation case at the district court level was a shameful episode in the history of American law.[4] Equally if not more shocking have been some of the voting cases: for example, and selecting almost at random, Judge Clayton's performance in the Bolivar County (Miss.) case.[5]

The judges in both cases cited had been for some years on the federal bench. The record of more recent appointees has, if anything, been worse. If one were to place on one side of the scale the enforcement activities of the Department of Justice from 1961 to the present, and on the other side the appointments made to the federal bench in the South by the Kennedy and Johnson administrations, the way the scale would tip would still be very questionable. We have put on the federal courts of the South for life tenure a succession of men who have made clear their opposition to declared rights of the constitution. One cannot read, to take another from all too many examples, the proceedings before Judge Cox of the Southern District of Mississippi in the contempt citation of attorney Jess

---

[4]*Bell* v. *Rippy,* 133 F. Supp. 811, 146 F. Supp. 455. *Borders* v. *Rippy,* 184 F. Supp. 402.

[5]See the United States' brief in *U.S.* v. *Lewis,* #20411 before the U.S.C.A. for the 5th Circuit, May 1963.

Brown without a feeling of complicity in what surely was a degradation of this country's government.[6]

Perhaps naturally, but still not excusably, some other federal jurisdictions have lately exhibited partiality for the other side. These include the Supreme Court of the United States. I find it just barely conceivable that the Supreme Court would not have reached an opposite decision in *Cox* v. *Louisiana*[7] had the plaintiff been of a different color. The dissent by Mr. Justice Black in that case seems to me overwhelming in its logic and cogent in its warning that "those who encourage minority groups to believe that the United States Constitution and federal laws give them a right to patrol and picket in the streets whenever they choose, in order to advance what they think to be a just and noble end, do no service to those minority groups, their cause, or their country."

There is the risk, too, that the federal courts may be overloaded and may attempt to do too much. In the long run this may well prove a greater problem than that of judicial partiality. In addition to the already heavy and novel functions placed on the

[6]*In the matter of R. Jess Brown*, Appellant, 346 Fed. 2d 903.
[7]379 US Ct. 559 (1965). This was a case arising from enforcement of a Louisiana statute punishing picketing before a courthouse. It is worth remarking that the majority of the court (*a*) found the statute constitutional and (*b*) rejected Cox's claims that the demonstration he led was not a clear and present danger to the judicial process and did not show evidence of intent to obstruct justice. The court reversed Cox's conviction by a finding that the police had given permission for an unlawful demonstration; the police denied on the record that any such permission had been given.

district courts by *Brown* v. *Topeka,* Congress in 1957 imposed on the courts the vexing and burdensome responsibility of ending voter discrimination. Well before 1960 it was apparent that the voting provisions of the act of 1957 were not efficiently designed to achieve their objective, and the U. S. Commission on Civil Rights in 1959 proposed new methods that would take the process out of the courts. Both the Eisenhower administration and Congress spurned that recommendation, and by the Civil Rights Act of 1960 added further chores on the courts. In 1964, when by this time the evidence was unmistakably clear to any diligent observer, Congress at the behest of the administration further retooled the judicial method of registering voters. As, I believe, an almost direct consequence, the country in early 1965 experienced the hard fact of Selma, and we now have finally in the Voting Rights Act of 1965 a statute which offers the first realistic opportunity of Negroes to register despite concerted community opposition, provided it be well used by the Department of Justice. The Voting Rights Act of 1965 recognizes something which through a marvel of perversity the Department of Justice and Congress in 1957, 1960, and 1964 refused to acknowledge. Voter registration is a purely ministerial act, a job for functionaries. It is a task which functionaries supported by a plain and explicit statute can effectively perform, but which august courts are not equipped to do.

Cases coming in increasing frequency to the federal courts raise another threat of overloading. These deal with so-called *de facto* school segregation or racial imbalance, and some cases from the South ask the federal courts for continual supervision of school desegregation plans. Some of these cases are necessary. Others show a worrisome predilection for legal rather than political action. The district court, for example, still retains jurisdiction in the Atlanta school case, and from time to time is pressed for further decrees. In the city of Atlanta every member of the school board is elected by city-wide vote, and roughly 40 percent of that vote is Negro. At points such as these, and at similar points occurring elsewhere and in regard to other matters, the Negro community needs to accept the fact of its own political power. It is hard to be concerned about the constitutional rights of a class amply equipped with power to defend its rights politically.

The *de facto* school cases have been, so far, quite gingerly stepped around by federal appellate courts, especially the Supreme Court. Sooner or later, however, some authoritative precedents certainly will be established. Judge Kaufman in the New Rochelle case[8] made a finding of fact that policies of the local school board had, over the years, systematically been designed to maximize school segregation and, therefore, ordered the school board to adopt policies that would be similarly systematically designed to minimize segregation. This seems to me a tenable position. Judge Kaufman's opinion appears to emphasize the motives behind past policies, and perhaps the emphasis should be on the clearly evident consequences of policies,

[8]*Taylor* v. *New Rochelle*, 195 F. Supp. 231.

without special regard to motives. But beyond this federal courts might well move only with caution.

What is involved here is the question of the use of legal redress in lieu of political influence and power to secure interests. *De facto* school segregation is a serious problem and remedies are imperative; it does not follow that the remedies should be applied by courts. This is precisely the sort of problem that requires the flexible, experimental, interest-balancing methods of legislative bodies, and appellate courts would do well to be wary of allowing themselves to be drawn into short-circuiting the political channels for change.

The essential point is, I think, that we recognize that interests rather than legal rights are at issue. Our courts, overly encouraged by zealous lawyers, have shown a disturbing tendency to forget the difference, and to presume that a legal right can be carved out of the constitutional corpus by persuasive identification of minority with public interests. It is both a logical and a political fallacy to contend that every valid minority interest implies an enforceable legal right for the individuals who comprise that minority.

The point is worthy of insistence, that what we do about schools is fundamentally important. This is so not merely because the country is spending vast sums of money and talent on education, and, one hopes may be spending even more, but because Plato was not wrong when he held that the education of the young was the primary function and responsibility of organized society. Whatever we do with the schools, we must do with the greatest care, searching both diligently and humbly for the deepest level of insight we can attain. No one can claim to have such insight, and that is part of the reason why the deliberations of a community are entitled to much respect.

Judicially declared rights are a mainstay of the American constitution. Traditionally, they have been invoked to remove a purposeful act of oppression against an individual or class of individuals. What is novel is for courts to declare that an individual has, as a member of a class, a right to a particular kind of social institution. Such declarations in the field of education may have for the present a rhetorical, even a theoretical, charm, but it is doubtful they have the stamina to restrict for long the urge of a democratic society constantly to shape and reshape its judgment about the good life, and the teaching of it.

It may be said that this is old-fashioned. Our contemporary American society is composed of a plurality of groups and classes, each of which must be made at home in the larger community. Therefore, it is argued, legally enforceable rights must be recognized against institutional practices offensive to any group and even, in some cases, rights must be recognized that require society to provide an institution in the form desired by a group.

It is at least questionable whether the conclusion follows from the premises, which are themselves perfectly valid. May it not be the case that precisely because ours is a pluralistic society we need most surely to rely on the give and take of the political process? Is it not, when open to the free participation of every citizen, a unifying force in a way in which the decrees and prohibitions of a court cannot be? At this uniquely historic time, when we are attempting the extraordinarily difficult task of building an integrated society, can we get on well with the job by curbing the freedom of school boards to experiment with methods and patiently to lead the way toward first one and then another consensus. Judicial decrees could desegregate; to integrate is a far different matter, and one that calls for political art.

Similar caution might warn that courts take on an imponderably complex task when they venture very far into the regulation of the religious and moral instruction of the young. The Supreme Court has been, during the last decade or so, a powerful defender of individual rights and liberties. This nation cannot afford to forget, however, that thirty years ago it became necessary for the Court to relinquish certain constitutional territory it had occupied, and return it to the legislatures of federal and state governments.

Speaking only of trends and without necessary reference to any particular cases, I think some reconsideration is prudent. Politics and religion have had to get along together since men first began to live in societies and to wonder about life and death. Theirs is an ancient family relationship, and though law must now and then mediate between them it cannot lastingly arbitrate their differences.

The field of public education—of the ways through which a society rears its children—is a proper field for legal rules which, as in *Brown* v. *Topeka*, simply declare that society must do for all as it does for some.

To insure such a result we need the rigidity of legal commands. The law trespasses at its own peril in fields far beyond. The place of religious instruction in the schools is not susceptible of simple or clear answers. It is all very well to forbid the state power to prescribe a prayer; this is a good ground rule, but it lies only at the gateway of much more deeply embedded, more subtle practices. We can well say that the policeman on the beat is not the authority to decide what is and is not obscene literature, but lawyers who think they can by constitutional norms usurp the community's instinctive feeling of responsibility for rearing the young are leading the law toward contempt. They are, moreover, encouraging in another and supremely vital field that sense of estrangement between the superstructure of an institution and its constituent body which is a fearsomely prevalent and growing feature of American social life.

I think no concerns, not even those of foreign relations, will test more strenuously the wisdom of the next generation of our public leadership than will those of our educational system and its practices. The most volatile of them is now that of race, and it likely will remain so. We have with us and ahead of us wretched and massive problems of equal educational opportunity for all children. If they are not overcome, we shall have failed in our time, as the men of a century ago did in theirs, to make of this one nation at peace with itself. But it is futile to attempt to solve these problems by the method of declaring and vesting legal rights to a certain kind of education. That road leads almost surely to the severe weakening of the public's sense of interest in and responsibility for the public schools.

Not every valid interest is a right, and the law should not allow itself to be persuaded to say so. We must, as any nation must, live as a people bound together by ties of mutual trust, not as a people armored against each other. To this end we have joined with generations of ancestors in creating what is the greatest work of man—liberal democracy. Democracy represents a huge faith that a people can in common process locate what for that people are the satisfying terms of social life. We can and should remove obstructions to the flow of that process, as we did, for example, by *Brown* v. *Topeka* and *Baker* v. *Carr.* But it is essentially undemocratic—and therefore corrupting of the process—for judge-made law to attempt to direct the flow by affirmative decree.

The liberal tradition is otherwise. To reinforce vested interests by fencing them in with legal rights was the strategy of laissez-faire capitalism—the strategy of ruling classes of all earlier times. Liberalism promised something different, an opposition to all vested interests, and in its present ascendancy that promise should not be repudiated.

Title VI of the Act of 1964 charges the U. S. Office of Education to withhold federal funds from school districts that subject persons to discrimination because of race or color. The statute as applied to Southern schools requires much skillful administration, but the legislative mandate is fairly clear. Far more complicated problems arise in those school districts where no overt policies of discrimination exist. Sec. 401 (b) of the Act warns the Office of Education away from problems of racial imbalance, but this warning is on the face of it not applicable to Title VI. The Office is obliged, therefore, to determine in the situation of Northern and Western schools what "subjected to discrimination" means.

Title VI was an extremely welcome enactment, both because of the forward thrust it imparts to Southern school desegregation and because it took much of the burden of effecting compliance away from the overstrained federal courts and put it into the hands of administrators. Nevertheless, because constitutional rights are claimable, the courts remain an available avenue of change. A reciprocal relationship between the executive and judicial departments is created: in framing their regulations, administrators will rely, and have so done, on the case law already existent; in framing their decrees, courts will in the future almost certainly be influenced by policies adopted by the Office of Education. In a recent order Judge Wisdom of the Fifth Circuit announced as much, and the present rule in the Fifth Circuit seems to be that the court in situations brought before it will not be satisfied by less progress than is required by the Office of Education.[9] It is probably a safe inference that it *will be* satisfied by what is acceptable to the Office.

If Judge Wisdom's rule is accepted in Northern and Western jurisdictions and retained in Southern

---

[9] *Singleton* v. *Jackson Municipal Separate School District,* 348 F. 2d 729.

jurisdictions when the characteristic problems there become, as they soon will, like those of the North and West, a very great responsibility will be put on the Office of Education. The academic community could on this point be of real service to the civil-rights movement, which is not always as well acquainted as it should be with the nature of federal bureaus and of their tendency to be conservative and protective of those whom they regulate. Were the civil-rights movement to pressure the Office of Education into taking to itself a prime responsibility for deciding how well local school boards cure racial imbalance, the results could be very disappointing.

It would seem wise for the Office of Education to take a limited view of its statutory assignment here, and wise for the civil-rights movement not to press it to do otherwise until a sufficient body of case law has been built up on the *de facto* problems; in short, the Office should not go faster than the courts.

If there are persuasive reasons for both federal courts and federal administration to be restrained in creating new legal rules and concepts for the schools, to whom should we look for change that is necessary? I think we should turn to legislative bodies, and in doing so remember where power and responsibility over the schools are primarily located, and that is with the state and local authorities. Inherently, they ought to be more responsive to liberal pressures than either federal courts or federal administrators. There can probably be, moreover, no stable solutions to these hard questions of racial imbalance that do not have the concurrence of the school boards. One would hope, therefore, that the first concern of urban parents, both Negro and white, will be to find ways to present their interests effectively through these channels. One would even more fervently hope that school authorities would come alive, or would be enabled by the political process to come alive. By and large, the political process has not worked well. That does not mean it cannot be made to work well. When citizens of a democracy lose confidence in the legislative process, they make a severe judgment about themselves and their skill at self-government. If in New York, Chicago, and many lesser cities political processes cannot be made to work better as to school problems, the alternative will almost certainly be, because pressures are so necessitous, federal regulation by courts or administrators, or else precipitate, clumsy local decisions to appease popular clamors.

Prior to 1957 there was virtually no office or person within the federal executive with a special or even a secondary concern for civil rights. In that year, the Commission on Civil Rights and the Civil Rights Division of the Department of Justice were created. By a remarkable series of executive orders and administrative actions, President Kennedy later built within every department and agency of the federal executive a sense of alertness to problems of discrimination, and he created several positive programs as well; this process has been ably continued by President Johnson.

Congress, by the Act of 1964, created two new agencies: the Equal Employment Opportunities Commission and the Community Relations Service of the Department of Commerce (now being transferred to

the Department of Justice). In addition, heavy responsibilities by statute or by executive order have
been assigned to the U. S. Office of Education and to
the Department of Labor in particular, as well as,
under Title VI of the Act of 1964, to all departments
and agencies of the government. As a huge employer
and even larger contractor, the Department of Defense especially influences the employment opportunities of Negroes. The U. S. Office of Economic Opportunity in administering and coordinating the antipoverty program is working day to day with problems
of race. State governments of the North and West and
many local governments have created and empow-
ered fair employment, fair housing, and other civil-
rights agencies. In addition, they are closely involved
in the antipoverty drive, especially by their relation-
ships with so-called Community Action Programs.

This is a remarkable institutionalizing of concern.
The cause of equal opportunities now has throughout
the political order strong spokesmen and that special
kind of vigilance and diligence which bureaucrats
impart to their assignments. The federal government's
civil-rights and antipoverty bureaucracy is, in fact, so
substantial at the present time that one of its keenest
problems is and will undoubtedly continue to be administrative disarray. A bureau for every problem, and
a string of bureaus for some, is an American technique
of government. For problems that will be with us
always, it is a satisfactory technique. At the risk of
seeming to cavil prematurely, one can point to the
dismal prospect that these civil-rights bureaus now in
being may never admit victory, that they may grow

old and rigid in the cause of civil rights long after that cause has changed.

Racial discrimination is a problem to be solved, not a problem to be endured. Grateful as we can be for the mobilization of this degree of governmental strength, we should even now be giving thought to the advantage of incorporating as much of this effort as we sensibly can into the normal administrative structures. The transfer of responsibility for enforcing equal employment opportunity among federal contractors from a presidential committee to the Department of Labor was a promising step, and the transfer to that Department of the functions of the new Equal Employment Opportunities Commission should be seriously considered. The Act of 1964 in effect allows and encourages state governments to preempt the fields of enforcing nondiscrimination in public accommodations and interstate employment, and this seems a wholesome use of the advantages of a federal system.[10]

I think that a sound general policy would be to move as efficiently and as quickly as possible to normalizing the federal concern for racial discrimination, so that enforcement of antidiscrimination would become as routine a matter as is, for example, enforcement of the child-labor or wage-and-hour standards. We should not assume that racial discrimination will be a permanent feature of social life. We should think of it as an ill to be treated by surgery, not everlasting medication. Indeed, to assume that discrimination will

[10] See sections 204 (c), 709 (b), and 1104 of the act.

live forever is to come altogether too close to conceding the moral argument to the segregationists.

After all these things are said, we can still hold that the prospects for federalism are good. The business of government is to govern well; that is, to provide the kind of order satisfying to the wants and wishes of a people. It is dangerous sentimentality to presuppose that the guarantee of such humane values inheres in any governmental form. If the federal system is not adaptable to the contemporary and emerging needs of American society it should be discarded with all deliberate speed. But I believe that it is adaptable. The Austinian doctrine of sovereignty, dear as it still is to lawyers, has been a monstrous fiction not only because of its moral treachery but because it simply has not corresponded with the facts of human society. No fictitious sovereign is able to dam up the human instinct to associate with like-minded persons and with persons of similar interests in combinations compact with authority and capable of furnishing direction for their adherents. The life of a modern democracy is far too complex for men to seek their social purposes within the confines of a single arena of decision-making. We need the lush, fluid growth of associations mediating government's force and conditioning its decision-making, providing so many additional arenas for ascertaining democracy's will. The argument of *Federalist 10* cuts in more than one way. The federal system can, Madison argued, curb the power of special interests better than could each state acting alone. The obverse is that the federal system can facilitate the free development of legitimate interests better than could a more centralized American government. Moreover, the fifty state governments are with us; the pragmatic thing to do is to put them to use.

Federalism, as an idea, should be taken out of the realm of legal fictions, It has been there too long already. Let us affirm flatly that the phrase "state rights" is meaningless; to the person who will not be convinced of this by the clear logic of events, let us simply affirm as a moral decision that only individuals have rights which the constitution must respect. Let us say further that there is no such thing as "state sovereignty," and let us be sensible enough to say that there never has been such a thing. We carry a lot of straw in our heads and sometimes we must sweep it out by such affirmations as these. And let us note, finally, that our emancipation from such enervating political superstitions is a triumph of liberalism.

Having been freed from the superstitions of federalism, we can try to make it work. I conceive that the republic is fortunately endowed by its heritage of so many governmental instruments available for use. Whether we entrust much or little governmental initiative and power to them depends on the wishes and policies of those same liberal forces which have at long last made possible a well-functioning federalism.

Federalism means more than the preservation of the hulks of the states, and more than the decentralization of administration. Federalism means the reservation to the states of some vital areas of political decision-making. It means the acceptance of some measure of variety in social values and modes of social control, so that there can be and may be certain characteristic differences in the quality of social life of Michigan as compared with New York, and other differences with Georgia or California. Federalism implies nonuniformity and implies it regarding not merely small but important matters as well.

Federalism implies, for example, that though the First Amendment's protections should be one thing and one thing only for the entire country, nonprotected forms of speech, such as pornography, could have various treatments, and the wisdom of the people of Illinois or of Wisconsin could be trusted to make valid yet unlike determinations that national courts would respect unless patently offensive to the First Amendment. Ascertaining what does and what does not appeal to prurient interest is, after all, at most a question of fact, not law; consistency of law throughout the republic does not require the assumption that the pruriency of our citizenry is of unvarying readiness from Maine to California. Federalism implies, to suggest another possibility, that the people of each state might debate for themselves and form a judgment as to the best coordination of public and sectarian school resources, without fear of reversal so long as no individual's right to worship in his own way were diminished nor no sect given an unwanted access to the mind of any child. Or, to suggest a third possibility, federalism implies that the states should continue to be able to adopt distinguishable policies and practices in the common endeavor for equal educational opportunity for all children, regardless of race.

What have we to fear from variety, from experimentation, from a multiplicity of efforts to find the most satisfying terms of a good life in society? Why must we be passionately fond of uniformity?

Liberals as well as conservatives are capable of doctrinaire rigidities. Southern conservatives made a demonic fetish of state rights; liberals can do the same with the slogan of a wall of separation between church and state. Southern conservatives could be blind to values that were morally imperative, such as equality; liberals can be blind to values that are the instructions of experience, such as local self-government.

Federalism is an eminently sensible form for a political order to adopt: no more than this can be said for it. But no more than this can be said for any form. In the situation of modern America it provides a chance to distribute governmental functions in ways that effectively represent the peoples' interests. Beyond this, federalism has its own attractions. It enables greater intimacy between leaders and constituents. It promises, if we wish them, communal variety and fecund talents. It is a form congenial to the liberal spirit and deserving of its advocacy.

V

★ ★ ★ ★ ★

Public Policy and the Art of Peacemaking

THE SPECIFIC and traditional forms of federalism are not to be despised, but neither are they of paramount value. All through the nation's history they have been altered and adjusted to meet public policies. Usually, we have approached these changes as questions of power: "Shall the national government have power to do so and so? Shall the power be with the states?" Whatever merit these old debates on the theme of power may have had, they are not now the framework for useful thought.

There is a vast qualitative difference between decentralized administration of national laws and policies and a commitment to federal units of government independent of Washington's supervision and direction. Do we have such a commitment? Are we agreeable to the nonuniformity that it implies? In economic matters I am not sure that we are or should be. If federalism still has worth to the American people, it is and will be because it serves a good purpose in reaching satisfying directions regarding our social culture. As America becomes more crowded and more self-critical, the questions of how we get along with each other become ever more vital. Is it not likely that we can respond to these questions in gentler and more humane fashion if we commit ourselves to the diversity and the greater intimacy of local and state decision-making?

Neither are the traditional articles of liberalism's fighting faith necessarily and permanently precious. Liberalism is the defense of the free mind of the individual against institutional domination. This is a never-ending danger, and liberty is always in jeopardy and needs to be secured. But the arena of struggle constantly changes. It is, for example, not enough for liberals to combat violations of civil rights by Southern state governments and wanton cruelty against Negroes by klansmen. These evils have not been the causes that have rendered the conditions of masses of Negroes more miserable today than they were a decade ago. Those causes have included at their forefront acts, even well-intentioned acts, of the federal government. Liberals are not accepting the responsibilities of rule when they enact and administer urban renewal and federal highway construction programs with but casual regard for their effects on housing supply and segregation, when they cut cotton acreage with no provision for displaced workers, or when they allow the Army to abandon its role as the indigents' schoolmaster by upping the literacy requirements for conscription.

Nor is it, for example, enough for liberals to be exercised about such details of social housekeeping as prayer recitals in schools or the free speech of the rarefied intelligentsia in the crevices of megalopolis. These interesting and appealing causes have little to do with what Whitehead meant when he said "the essence of freedom is the practicability of purpose."[1] More to the point are conditions that today threaten a free science, liberalism's own child, and trade unions and professional associations, both nurtured by its teachings. It ought to be of primary concern that science puts itself steadily more at the service of political policies and that brains and investigative resources are increasingly monopolized by a few public and private institutions; it ought to be of equal concern that unions and professional associations all too often are barriers to individuals on the outside and creators and defenders of special privileges that frustrate public needs. To be alert to basic problems such as these is to be mindful of responsibilities of rule.

The old agenda of liberalism is now virtually complete, made so by the civil-rights and reapportionment victories. It was an agenda primarily devoted to completing the democratization of this country.

The new agenda has to do with making a better civilization—with deepening the civility of our life and its institutions. It is an agenda of inescapable needs, and the main question is whether the liberal forces which now rule this country will assume it or whether the liberal consensus will fragment before it and, after

[1] *Adventure of Ideas* (New York: Macmillan, 1933), p. 84.

a time of frustration and confusion, some new grouping of right or left will manage the country's will. Between liberals and radicals of left or right there is always a basic distrust. Succinctly put, the liberal suspects the radical would not use power liberally—that is, with respect for individual freedom—and the radical knows that the liberal shies away from radical reform.

So let it be; it has always been. The liberal is skeptical of all alleged truth and, consequently, of all radical solutions to social problems. He cannot, however, be anything but vigorously responsive to the reality and dimension of social issues that have come up from the roots, because if he is not the issues will loosen the always tenuous grip that a society has on individual freedom. Such issues make up the new, the civility-imparting agenda of the republic.

This agenda includes, and the recital is familiar, the complications of our mismanaged and overgrown cities, with their problems of poverty, of crowding that stultifies individual growth and expression, of ugliness; the awesome issues of the controlled use of science in the interest of humanity, defending the richness of life against hideous weaponry and strengthening it rather than cursing it by man-displacing machines; the fratricidal strain of an international state-system pounded by a sudden torrent of new states, intolerant political doctrines, and virulent emotions.

The republic is better prepared to confront and deal constructively with all this than it was before the Negro revolt. Its head is clearer and more reflective, new talents are available, the hampering veto power of the South is ended. Yet the real constitution of the republic contains a large residue of its ancient instability. This is still a country in which race is a negotiable asset.

What we had to learn in the past we should not have to rediscover at some sad future national crisis. Race is a problem that must be confronted directly. It does not solve itself as a byproduct of advance on other problems. That has always been a wistful hope—always disappointed. Rather than yielding to indirect policies, race confounds and often defeats the possibility of constructive action on other problems. It is very doubtful that the new agenda of our needs can be well met until this becomes in fact as in law a republic of equals.

And so I speak of peace-making. This implies that we recognize with candor and depth of understanding that there is division and conflict and that terms of peace must be found. By all the evidence the situation of Negro Americans is presently so harsh that to overstate it is hard. Probably no domestic concern has ever been dealt with in graver terms by a President than in Mr. Johnson's two speeches of March 15 and June 4, 1965. The second, given at Howard University, was a remarkable statement, both for its content and as a historic event. Since its delivery there is little anyone can add or needs to add to draw attention to the severity of the national problems and the widespread misery of Negro Americans.

Mr. Johnson in that address also voiced a new ideal, one so novel that it represents a changed direction of political philosophy:

We seek not just freedom but opportunity.
We seek not just legal equity but human ability.
Not just equality as a right and a theory
but equality as a fact and equality as a result.
To this end equal opportunity is essential, but
not enough, not enough.[2]

For a President to say this made of the day an
occasion of first-rank historic magnitude. Obviously,
the President's language was loose: the phrase "equality as a fact and equality as a result" is not clearly
intelligible either in thought or conceived application.
We do well to perceive in his words, however, a groping of the national will toward a society which will
have a care to see that each individual is purposively
enabled to act at the highest level of his innate talents.

To achieve such a breath-taking (but also en-
nobling) goal will require economic and educational
policies of the utmost soundness. They will but doubt-
fully succeed, however, unless *first of all* racial peace
is established. To do that requires public policies that
prepare the ground for reconciliation at the heart of
white and Negro Americans. Of the proposals that
follow, none is original. They embrace, by what they
include and also by what they exclude, terms of public
peace and realistic progress.

Of primary importance is the security of the person. People need not live in fear. Since December 3,
1955, as many as eighty-four killings in the South have
been connected with the civil-rights drive; thirty of

[2] Italics supplied.

these were in 1964–65. No deference to the forms of federalism can allow this to continue. The primary obligation of every government is to preserve the peace and public safety.

Thirty-four persons were killed in the Watts section of Los Angeles in less than a week of the summer of 1965. Most of these were Negroes, and most apparently were killed by law-enforcement agents: more killings occurred in just a few days than throughout the South in nearly two years. This can remind us of what has been one of the pertinent features of the civil-rights struggle since 1954. Compared with earlier periods of racial tension in the United States, it has been fairly bloodless; the racial riots after World War I, for example, caused far more deaths than we have seen. Earlier American race struggles all too frequently brought into being white mobs. We have had these again, but they have been typically different. The white mob has not lately been an offensive force, coursing through Negro quarters and frenziedly bent on destruction and death; that work has been left to small bands of furtive men. In the South the white mob has been a defensive force, and in the North no white mob has yet formed, as in East St. Louis, Chicago, and Washington in World War I days.

No Negro mob has really appeared in the South; in the North and West it has, marking possibly one of the first times in history that the initial mob has been black instead of white.

The apparent step-up of civil-rights killings in the South during the last two or three years, combined with the new aggressiveness of Negroes in non-Southern ghettos, is a plain warning. Unless personal security is assured, the way of nonviolence among Negro Southerners will be replaced by retaliatory violence and possibly mob muscle. The inhabitants of Northern and Western ghettos continue to endure the misery they have long known. For years their anticipation of change has been sharpened and made sensitive, yet they have seen little improvement in their lives. Disappointed expectations turn misery to aggression.

Beyond securing the right to live, the job of erasing all racial barriers must be completed. We are well along in ending segregation and discrimination by law, though some forms still remain. The most important of the laws yet to be eliminated is the prohibition against interracial marriages prevailing throughout the South and in some other states as well.

Law is not the only authority that regulates our lives. Extralegal powers are often of comparable importance. Real estate bodies and mortgage firms, employers, professions, and trade unions establish and enforce discriminatory rules that affect and often determine where persons may live and how well they get on. We have not made nearly enough headway in ending housing and employment discrimination, even though both state and federal regulation is being applied.

We should have as our goal—and the touchstone for policies of government and also of concerned private groups—the strengthening of the individual.

This is a matter of semantics, but is necessary if we are to approach our needs with clear heads and intelligent actions. Integrated education, for example, is not a value in itself. The goal must be the better education of all our children; to that purpose and in the interests of white as well as Negro children, integration is a valued aid. We simply cannot, however, measure the quality of education if we elevate racial integration to preeminent rank among values. Moreover, realism suggests that, although we should expect school boards to draw their attendance lines, locate their buildings, and assign their faculty in such a way as to give the children the maximum advantages of racial association, we ought not expect the schools to compensate for all the evils inherent in housing segregation.

There may be more point to saying that integrated housing is an end in itself, because, whereas education is only a means to knowledge and skills, a home is, or one would think should be, an end. Certainly, the twin disgrace of slums and restricted neighborhoods are intertwined with every problem of race that confronts us.

We should study as seriously as we can what the governmental housing policies are that can effectively dispel the slums and curb neighborhood exclusiveness. If the study leads to it, we should not be reluctant to impose criminal penalties on realtors, lenders, or landlords who conspire to maintain either, for what they perpetuate is the suffocation of human beings through filth and hopelessness. There is possibly little we can or should do to limit free choice in the housing market, but we can insure that the choices are freely made and are not coerced, however stealthily, by the housing industry.

Terms of peace cannot be unilaterally prepared, no matter how much good will may accompany the effort. A third requirement depends as much on Negro leadership as on that of the white community or governing power. Negroes must enter into full and free participation in politics at all levels. As I have said before, this seems an indispensable condition of racial peace. Voting is no panacea; the ballot is not a draft on the bank of social gains. But the empirical fact is that no steady Negro advance has been achieved in any Southern community in which Negroes do not vote in politically significant numbers.

Beyond voter registration is actual use of the ballot in elections. Beyond voting, both in North and South, is the sophisticated organization of political power. Concurrent with that is candidacy for office, and candidacy not merely or even most importantly from predominantly Negro constituencies but—by the use of political bargaining power to lay the base for electing Negroes—from mixed constituencies. These are primarily tasks for Negroes themselves to accomplish. Others can be of useful assistance, but the prime responsibility for skillfully developing and using their political power rests with the Negro communities. For a long time to come the country will be affected for good or ill by whether Negroes from their own resources can transfer to political organization the same high qualities of leadership they have supplied for the civil-rights movement.

Political participation is not confined to legislative and executive offices. Negroes will have to be concerned, just as other ethnic groups have been, with representation throughout the full range of the political process. For example, an almost thoroughly white part of the government is the court system—from top to bottom and in federal as well as state jurisdictions. For another example, only very few Negroes in any section of the country sit on the boards, commissions, and committees which deal with urban renewal and city planning and zoning, subjects which are of immediate and vital concern to the Negro populace.

A further need is the systematic insertion [3] of Negroes into all the channels of professional and economic advancement. The word "systematic" implies that this should be done deliberately, because—Negroes having been for so long systematically kept out —common sense as well as simple justice requires a deliberate effort. The term "systematc insertion" implies something less than would the term "systematic integration."

It is now commonplace for businesses, government agencies, universities, and other institutions to expend time and money in recruiting "their Negro," their showcase exhibit or exhibits of nonprejudice. Smile at this as we may, it is nevertheless worthwhile. Although there is the constant danger that the endeavor will stop with the token acquisition, the equally likely result is that the way will have been opened for appreciable if slow increase. No handicap that Negroes presently carry is heavier than the feeling of hopelessness that holds down aspirations and discourages sustained effort. One helpful remedy is to provide

---

[3] I have borrowed the word from Professor Ernst Borinski of Tougaloo College.

younger Negro men and women, but particularly men, with the example of acceptance of other Negroes in places and positions formerly closed.

This implies that in some important areas institutions must adapt themselves to the need. For example, do universities have the social right at this time to regard their admission criteria as sacrosanct? Society has no very strong interest in what goes into a university; its main interest is with what comes out. There are now moves on the campus toward relaxing admission requirements for disadvantaged youth, just as industry is also hiring below stated qualifications. In both situations—that of the university and that of industry—the institution assumes a portion of responsibility for correcting the social neglect that produced disadvantage. Extreme and knowing care must be taken to respect the dignity of those who require special guidance and training, and the universities have a social obligation not to lower or dilute their exit criteria, just as industry has a responsibility not to lower its product standards.

We need not take seriously the accusation of favoritism when we encourage special programs in behalf of Negroes. Most white people who have got along well have been the recipients of many favors. High offices in Washington are widely filled by men whose most obvious qualification for preferment is that they are sons of fathers, brothers of brothers, or nephews of uncles, and the same is true throughout business and the professions and even the arts, and in some labor unions the practice is made formal. Negroes do not as yet have this advantage, nor are they in the chain of gossip which provides both early information about openings and recommendations. When the typical firm or university department or newspaper editor wants to take on a new man, someone calls his friends in the profession; this is the way most important appointments are made, and Negroes are as yet outside the circuit. Large companies tend to promote from within, and Negroes are not in the line of advance. It is not favoritism to build into our practices some *ad hoc* compensating bias.

Finally, as an essential to racial peace there needs to be a substantial strengthening of Negro community life. It is sometimes held against Negroes that they have not knitted as fully as have some other ethnic minorities a fabric of social organization. Considering their unique cultural short-changing, and considering also that they have put most of their attention and effort to the building of churches and colleges and that these same churches and colleges have been the base of the Negro revolt, the charge is not accurate or fair. But for moving beyond where they are, the Negro communities now need a rapid development of inner organization.

They are woefully short of capital. Only in a few places, such as Atlanta, Houston, and Durham, are there socially important concentrations of money within and for the benefit of the Negro community. They are short on their own welfare institutions, such as orphanages and homes for the aged. They are short on their own credit unions, charitable foundations, recreation centers, and just about everything.

To say this presents questions that confuse. The

civil-rights movement has proclaimed the goal of integration, not the goal of communal development. This has been the source of its appeal to hearts. Just as we have been contaminated by the brutality of Hitler or Stalin and the wanton war tactics of our time, so we have regained some of our humanity by living in the clean thought and faith of those who came singing, "black and white together." Negroes have said, let us integrate, which is to say, let us be reconciled one with another. In a deep way the philosophy of nonviolence is a beautiful expression of love. To many people it has been like a new gospel, which like the earlier gospel was to be a covenant of peace among men.

So with caution one points to the desirability of strengthening Negro communal life, for fear of violating a spirit that is fine and priceless. Yet I think we must do so, being careful to bear in mind that the purpose must not be communal separation but the better care and cultivation of individuals for full participation in an open society—and that is a better term, really, than integrated society. None of us, including the Negro leadership, is quite sure what the latter means. What we want is a society corresponding to the old democratic ideals, of each man counting for one and no man for more than one, and of all careers open to talent. This would be as near as we can likely come to an integrated society, with every man having the chance to find his level and be at peace with his neighbor. We cannot have it, however, or even come close to it unless talents are formed and each man learns to count himself of equal worth to all others.

We must start from where we are. And where we are is with good assets as well as crushing hardships. Difficult as it is to exaggerate the bitter facts of Negro poverty, we are unfair if we talk only in those terms. The Negro community has a substantial layer of talented leadership. It has a stable and growing middle class. Because society has not allowed this middle class to be free of segregation and discrimination, its further advance is linked to the elevation of all Negroes. This accounts, in fact, for much of the impetus behind the Negro revolt, for there is nothing on earth more revolutionary than a frustrated middle class. It is also our chief asset, for without the resources of leadership and stability within this Negro middle class, the prospects would be discouraging indeed.

We have a huge minority of depressed people, leavened by many who are not, who must grow toward competence and self-respect and further advancement along side each other, because there is no other way. Since community strength is so necessary, we should be willing to ask some unpleasant questions: Does the Negro community need another white social worker as much as it needs, as a small business loan, the money his or her education cost? Should we ever again build a large public-housing project within or close to an all Negro neighborhood, knowing in advance that it would add to already weak community cohesiveness? Should we bus children in large numbers away from Negro neighborhoods, thus weakening the influence of the school as a community center? Should there be any white policemen in Negro neighborhoods? (How many Italian policemen ever patrolled the Irish beats?)

I have tried here to suggest articles of peace: protection of the public peace, all barriers erased for the individual, active participation by Negroes in political life, the systematic insertion of Negroes into all avenues of economic advancement, public policies that never impede and encourage when they can the invigoration of Negro community life. Without adequate governmental programs of economic stimulus and educational improvement, there will be no peace on any terms. But unless we know what is a viable settlement, programs however massive will miss their mark.

Americans have a long record of winning wars. The question is not so much whether we shall win the war against the old patterns of discrimination. We shall. The more urgent question is whether we shall win the peace, for America has more than once botched the peace that followed successful wars. The old patterns of discrimination and segregation are on their way to discard. The new patterns will either bring us peace or another war.

The grand endeavor we are now engaged in to end both poverty and discrimination has been made necessary by one fact only, and that is the desperate conditions we had allowed to grow within American democracy. Not surprisingly, some Negro intellectuals, joined by some whites, view these conditions as being the true measure of the nation. One spokesman said not long ago, in the context of a speech against our presence in Vietnam: "Negroes, better than anyone

else, are in a position to question the war—not because
they understand the war better but because they
better understand the United States."

Is it so, that the hard-rock truth about any society
is the aggression that comes out of its subconscious?
What, after all, is America? Is it, in its most characteristic essense, the nation that exterminated red
men and enslaved and then degraded black men? Are
these acts our truth, the real face of our true selves?
I think not. They are sins as vile and as heavy as any
perpetrated by Bolsheviks or Afrikaaners, and we
shall not soon expiate them nor atone for them. But
the essential America has been and is a nation open
to the working of the liberal spirit, and, because it is,
the vision of atonement need not be an illusion.

One of the separations between whites and Negroes is lack of common folk heroes. I do not see, for
instance, how any Negro could have much respect for
the memory of Woodrow Wilson or Andrew Jackson,
and he must feel at most a detached tolerance for such
more venerable figures as Washington and Jefferson.
Lincoln must be at this time very nearly the only uni-
versal hero. Perhaps it is in his spirit of unwavering
resolve, of refusal to bear malice or to succumb to
arrogance, of compassionate acceptance of human
frailty that we can now make peace and join ourselves
in a single nation.

The new voice of Negro Americans adds new
items to the liberal agenda. The era which began in
the dark depression of the 1930's and which has accomplished all it set out to do cannot now end quietly.
Civil rights for Negroes was on the liberal agenda from

the beginning, though fairly far down. But the challenge to build an integrated society without poverty was not something liberalism had seriously thought about. So it was an epochal moment last June when President Johnson declared that equal opportunity is not enough, that we seek equality as a fact and a result. The question is whether liberalism will achieve this in our day, or whether it will fail and some other era in the future will have to accomplish it.

Our best hope for success is through public policies grounded in pragmatism. This implies a skeptical wariness toward neat solutions reminiscent of the Townsendite and technocrat proposals of the 1930's. It implies also a refusal to romanticize. A depressing development in the radical wing of the civil-rights movement—which has always been a singing movement and has drawn its courage from song—has been the shift away from the grandeur of the old protest songs to new ones that can charitably be described only as enthroning in their words the eternal sophomore done usually to music like that of a Pentecostal revival meeting. The civil-rights movement was founded on protest, but not protest as a way of life. It and its allies should take some thought against making protest another opportunistic fad. The exhibitionist is a pariah, and exhibitionist protest is the intruder, fouling the dream of those who made a revolution.

But if our policies need to be pragmatic, they ought also to be purposeful. One tension within the civil-rights movement has been between those to whom nonviolence is a philosophical or religious commitment and those to whom it is merely a useful technique. Our sympathies and admiration belong to the former group, but toward the pragmatic bias of liberalism our stand should be reversed. Pragmatic policy is only a serviceable technique, not an expression of men's goals and purposes. Liberals need to open their minds to the pounding search impelled forward by the civil-rights movement, an adventure into the intimacy of life for social truth that can bring the peace of mutual forgiveness to individuals who must share the same moment of time and earthly place.

Over and beyond the contour of legal rights is another one more germane to human needs: the right of an individual to be a person, secure in his own individuality. In its fumbling and incomplete way, the South has known this, and to each of *its own* it has been inclined to acknowledge title deeds to a piece of cosmic real estate, a grant to a rightful place, having nothing to do with individual deserts. The youth of the civil-rights movement seem to be groping toward a similar though cleaner view. They seem to be saying that we need to accept each other: not love each other, not acknowledge each other's rights but— a much harder thing—accept: accept each as a creation that needs no justification other men can give.

The civil-rights fight has taught some hard things. We were shown the ugly face of violence and made to recognize it as our own. We were made to see all of America from the perspective of Negroes in Mississippi and Watts. This has been self-examination of the most necessary but severe kind. But we must not mistake insights for facts. We do not know ourselves unless we do look clearly into the face of Mississippi, but America whole is not Mississippi nor is it Watts. It is a splendid land, which belongs to its people and which they must care for.

Mr. James Baldwin has written: "No curtain under heaven is heavier than that curtain of guilt and lies behind which white Americans hide. That curtain may prove to be yet more deadly to the lives of human beings than that Iron Curtain which we speak of so much, and know so little."[4] This is not true. Courage means, by and large, to do one's job, and the courage asked of the intellectual is to respect facts and to seek wisdom. To view and judge America from the perspective of Mississippi or Harlem, and only in that way, is to distort. It is also to denigrate the Negroes' own great work. For white America no longer hides behind wrongdoing and lies precisely because the Negro revolt made us uncover ourselves.

It has been a trying but exhilarating period of self-discovery. The sin that America took to itself in its childhood, which it has endured and indulged all the years since, is being brought out. This country will never be the same again. Within the ceaseless flow of democracy, a new political agenda is being formed. How well will liberals fulfill the responsibilities of rule? How successfully will they apply their old talents of social criticism to self-evaluation? How courageous will they be at peace-making that protects the democratic victories won through the civil-rights movement?

[4]"The White Man's Guilt," *Ebony*, August, 1965, p. 48.

The Negro revolt at its best had a purity of thought and purpose we were not used to. It tore off our surfaces. Erudite college professors and sophisticated big city lawyers went South to join hands with illiterate Negroes and sing "We Shall Overcome." From the President down, we sang and we said, we shall overcome. The revolt rolled in with a single cry that was also its total program: "Freedom." What freedom? What does it mean? It was an overpowering revolutionary myth. Let us hope that the call for freedom will not die, because it purified. But let us get beyond the call and make enough freedom in this land for everyone.

Index

DATE DUE

DE 4 '70			
MR 16 81			
GAYLORD			PRINTED IN U.S.A.